ALBANIAN
VOCABULARY

FOR ENGLISH SPEAKERS

ENGLISH-
ALBANIAN

The most useful words
To expand your lexicon and sharpen
your language skills

3000 words

Albanian vocabulary for English speakers - 3000 words
By Andrey Taranov

T&P Books vocabularies are intended for helping you learn, memorize and review foreign words. The dictionary is divided into themes, covering all major spheres of everyday activities, business, science, culture, etc.

The process of learning words using T&P Books' theme-based dictionaries gives you the following advantages:

- Correctly grouped source information predetermines success at subsequent stages of word memorization
- Availability of words derived from the same root allowing memorization of word units (rather than separate words)
- Small units of words facilitate the process of establishing associative links needed for consolidation of vocabulary
- Level of language knowledge can be estimated by the number of learned words

T&P Books Publishing
www.tpbooks.com

ISBN: 978-1-78767-013-6

This book is also available in E-book formats.
Please visit www.tpbooks.com or the major online bookstores.

ALBANIAN VOCABULARY
for English speakers

T&P Books vocabularies are intended to help you learn, memorize, and review foreign words. The vocabulary contains over 3000 commonly used words arranged thematically.

- Vocabulary contains the most commonly used words
- Recommended as an addition to any language course
- Meets the needs of beginners and advanced learners of foreign languages
- Convenient for daily use, revision sessions, and self-testing activities
- Allows you to assess your vocabulary

Special features of the vocabulary

- Words are organized according to their meaning, not alphabetically
- Words are presented in three columns to facilitate the reviewing and self-testing processes
- Words in groups are divided into small blocks to facilitate the learning process
- The vocabulary offers a convenient and simple transcription of each foreign word

The vocabulary has 101 topics including:

Basic Concepts, Numbers, Colors, Months, Seasons, Units of Measurement, Clothing & Accessories, Food & Nutrition, Restaurant, Family Members, Relatives, Character, Feelings, Emotions, Diseases, City, Town, Sightseeing, Shopping, Money, House, Home, Office, Working in the Office, Import & Export, Marketing, Job Search, Sports, Education, Computer, Internet, Tools, Nature, Countries, Nationalities and more ...

T&P BOOKS' THEME-BASED DICTIONARIES

The Correct System for Memorizing Foreign Words

Acquiring vocabulary is one of the most important elements of learning a foreign language, because words allow us to express our thoughts, ask questions, and provide answers. An inadequate vocabulary can impede communication with a foreigner and make it difficult to understand a book or movie well.

The pace of activity in all spheres of modern life, including the learning of modern languages, has increased. Today, we need to memorize large amounts of information (grammar rules, foreign words, etc.) within a short period. However, this does not need to be difficult. All you need to do is to choose the right training materials, learn a few special techniques, and develop your individual training system.

Having a system is critical to the process of language learning. Many people fail to succeed in this regard; they cannot master a foreign language because they fail to follow a system comprised of selecting materials, organizing lessons, arranging new words to be learned, and so on. The lack of a system causes confusion and eventually, lowers self-confidence.

T&P Books' theme-based dictionaries can be included in the list of elements needed for creating an effective system for learning foreign words. These dictionaries were specially developed for learning purposes and are meant to help students effectively memorize words and expand their vocabulary.

Generally speaking, the process of learning words consists of three main elements:

- Reception (creation or acquisition) of a training material, such as a word list
- Work aimed at memorizing new words
- Work aimed at reviewing the learned words, such as self-testing

All three elements are equally important since they determine the quality of work and the final result. All three processes require certain skills and a well-thought-out approach.

New words are often encountered quite randomly when learning a foreign language and it may be difficult to include them all in a unified list. As a result, these words remain written on scraps of paper, in book margins, textbooks, and so on. In order to systematize such words, we have to create and continually update a "book of new words." A paper notebook, a netbook, or a tablet PC can be used for these purposes.

This "book of new words" will be your personal, unique list of words. However, it will only contain the words that you came across during the learning process. For example, you might have written down the words "Sunday," "Tuesday," and "Friday." However, there are additional words for days of the week, for example, "Saturday," that are missing, and your list of words would be incomplete. Using a theme dictionary, in addition to the "book of new words," is a reasonable solution to this problem.

The theme-based dictionary may serve as the basis for expanding your vocabulary.

It will be your big "book of new words" containing the most frequently used words of a foreign language already included. There are quite a few theme-based dictionaries available, and you should ensure that you make the right choice in order to get the maximum benefit from your purchase.

Therefore, we suggest using theme-based dictionaries from T&P Books Publishing as an aid to learning foreign words. Our books are specially developed for effective use in the sphere of vocabulary systematization, expansion and review.

Theme-based dictionaries are not a magical solution to learning new words. However, they can serve as your main database to aid foreign-language acquisition. Apart from theme dictionaries, you can have copybooks for writing down new words, flash cards, glossaries for various texts, as well as other resources; however, a good theme dictionary will always remain your primary collection of words.

T&P Books' theme-based dictionaries are specialty books that contain the most frequently used words in a language.

The main characteristic of such dictionaries is the division of words into themes. For example, the *City* theme contains the words "street," "crossroads," "square," "fountain," and so on. The *Talking* theme might contain words like "to talk," "to ask," "question," and "answer".

All the words in a theme are divided into smaller units, each comprising 3–5 words. Such an arrangement improves the perception of words and makes the learning process less tiresome. Each unit contains a selection of words with similar meanings or identical roots. This allows you to learn words in small groups and establish other associative links that have a positive effect on memorization.

The words on each page are placed in three columns: a word in your native language, its translation, and its transcription. Such positioning allows for the use of techniques for effective memorization. After closing the translation column, you can flip through and review foreign words, and vice versa. "This is an easy and convenient method of review – one that we recommend you do often."

Our theme-based dictionaries contain transcriptions for all the foreign words. Unfortunately, none of the existing transcriptions are able to convey the exact nuances of foreign pronunciation. That is why we recommend using the transcriptions only as a supplementary learning aid. Correct pronunciation can only be acquired with the help of sound. Therefore our collection includes audio theme-based dictionaries.

The process of learning words using T&P Books' theme-based dictionaries gives you the following advantages:

- You have correctly grouped source information, which predetermines your success at subsequent stages of word memorization
- Availability of words derived from the same root (lazy, lazily, lazybones), allowing you to memorize word units instead of separate words
- Small units of words facilitate the process of establishing associative links needed for consolidation of vocabulary
- You can estimate the number of learned words and hence your level of language knowledge
- The dictionary allows for the creation of an effective and high-quality revision process
- You can revise certain themes several times, modifying the revision methods and techniques
- Audio versions of the dictionaries help you to work out the pronunciation of words and develop your skills of auditory word perception

The T&P Books' theme-based dictionaries are offered in several variants differing in the number of words: 1.500, 3.000, 5.000, 7.000, and 9.000 words. There are also dictionaries containing 15,000 words for some language combinations. Your choice of dictionary will depend on your knowledge level and goals.

We sincerely believe that our dictionaries will become your trusty assistant in learning foreign languages and will allow you to easily acquire the necessary vocabulary.

TABLE OF CONTENTS

PERSONAL INFORMATION. FAMILY

HUMAN BODY. MEDICINE

APARTMENT

THE EARTH. WEATHER

PRONUNCIATION GUIDE

T&P phonetic alphabet	Albanian example	English example
[a]	flas [flas]	shorter than in ask
[e], [ɛ]	melodi [mɛlodí]	absent, pet
[ə]	kërkoj [kərkój]	driver, teacher
[i]	pikë [píkə]	shorter than in feet
[o]	motor [motór]	pod, John
[u]	fuqi [fucí]	book
[y]	myshk [myʃk]	fuel, tuna
[b]	brakë [brákə]	baby, book
[c]	oqean [ocɛán]	Irish - ceist
[d]	adoptoj [adoptój]	day, doctor
[ʣ]	lexoj [lɛdzój]	beads, kids
[ʤ]	xham [dʒam]	joke, general
[ð]	dhomë [ðómə]	weather, together
[f]	i fortë [i fórtə]	face, food
[g]	bullgari [buɫgarí]	game, gold
[h]	jaht [jáht]	home, have
[j]	hyrje [hýɾjɛ]	yes, New York
[ɟ]	zgjedh [zɟɛð]	geese
[k]	korik [korík]	clock, kiss
[l]	lëviz [ləvíz]	lace, people
[ɫ]	shkallë [ʃkáɫə]	feel
[m]	medalje [mɛdáljɛ]	magic, milk
[n]	klan [klan]	name, normal
[ɲ]	spanjoll [spaɲóɫ]	canyon, new
[ŋ]	trung [truŋ]	ring
[p]	polici [politsí]	pencil, private
[r]	i erët [i érət]	rice, radio
[ɾ]	groshë [grófʃə]	Spanish - pero
[s]	spital [spitál]	city, boss
[ʃ]	shes [ʃɛs]	machine, shark
[t]	tapet [tapét]	tourist, trip
[ts]	batica [batítsa]	cats, tsetse fly
[tʃ]	kaçube [katʃúbɛ]	church, French
[v]	javor [javór]	very, river
[z]	horizont [horizónt]	zebra, please
[ʒ]	kuzhinë [kuʒínə]	forge, pleasure
[θ]	përkthej [pərkθéj]	month, tooth

ABBREVIATIONS
used in the vocabulary

English abbreviations

ab.	-	about
adj	-	adjective
adv	-	adverb
anim.	-	animate
as adj	-	attributive noun used as adjective
e.g.	-	for example
etc.	-	et cetera
fam.	-	familiar
fem.	-	feminine
form.	-	formal
inanim.	-	inanimate
masc.	-	masculine
math	-	mathematics
mil.	-	military
n	-	noun
pl	-	plural
pron.	-	pronoun
sb	-	somebody
sing.	-	singular
sth	-	something
v aux	-	auxiliary verb
vi	-	intransitive verb
vi, vt	-	intransitive, transitive verb
vt	-	transitive verb

Albanian abbreviations

f	-	feminine noun
m	-	masculine noun
pl	-	plural

BASIC CONCEPTS

1. Pronouns

I, me	**Unë, mua**	[unə], [múa]
you	**ti, ty**	[ti], [ty]
he	**ai**	[aí]
she	**ajo**	[ajó]
it	**ai**	[aí]
we	**ne**	[nɛ]
you (to a group)	**ju**	[ju]
they (masc.)	**ata**	[atá]
they (fem.)	**ato**	[ató]

2. Greetings. Salutations

Hello! (fam.)	**Përshëndetje!**	[pərʃəndétjɛ!]
Hello! (form.)	**Përshëndetje!**	[pərʃəndétjɛ!]
Good morning!	**Mirëmëngjes!**	[mirəmənɟés!]
Good afternoon!	**Mirëdita!**	[mirədíta!]
Good evening!	**Mirëmbrëma!**	[mirəmbréma!]
to say hello	**përshëndes**	[pərʃəndés]
Hi! (hello)	**Ç'kemi!**	[tʃ'kémi!]
greeting (n)	**përshëndetje** (f)	[pərʃəndétjɛ]
to greet (vt)	**përshëndes**	[pərʃəndés]
How are you? (form.)	**Si jeni?**	[si jéni?]
How are you? (fam.)	**Si je?**	[si jɛ?]
What's new?	**Çfarë ka të re?**	[tʃfárə ká tə ré?]
Goodbye!	**Mirupafshim!**	[mirupáfʃim!]
Bye!	**U pafshim!**	[u páfʃim!]
See you soon!	**Shihemi së shpejti!**	[ʃíhɛmi sə ʃpéjti!]
Farewell!	**Lamtumirë!**	[lamtumírə!]
to say goodbye	**përshëndetem**	[pərʃəndétɛm]
So long!	**Tungjatjeta!**	[tunɟatjéta!]
Thank you!	**Faleminderit!**	[falɛmindérit!]
Thank you very much!	**Faleminderit shumë!**	[falɛmindérit ʃúmə!]
You're welcome	**Të lutem**	[tə lútɛm]
Don't mention it!	**Asgjë!**	[asɟé!]

It was nothing	**Asgjë**	[asɟé]
Excuse me! (fam.)	**Më fal!**	[mə fal!]
Excuse me! (form.)	**Më falni!**	[mə fálni!]
to excuse (forgive)	**fal**	[fal]

to apologize (vi)	**kërkoj falje**	[kərkój fáljɛ]
My apologies	**Kërkoj ndjesë**	[kərkój ndjésə]
I'm sorry!	**Më vjen keq!**	[mə vjɛn kɛc!]
to forgive (vt)	**fal**	[fal]
It's okay! (that's all right)	**S'ka gjë!**	[s'ka ɟə!]
please (adv)	**të lutem**	[tə lútɛm]

Don't forget!	**Mos harro!**	[mos haró!]
Certainly!	**Sigurisht!**	[siguríʃt!]
Of course not!	**Sigurisht që jo!**	[siguríʃt cə jo!]
Okay! (I agree)	**Në rregull!**	[nə réguɫ!]
That's enough!	**Mjafton!**	[mjaftón!]

3. Questions

Who?	**Kush?**	[kuʃ?]
What?	**Çka?**	[tʃká?]
Where? (at, in)	**Ku?**	[ku?]
Where (to)?	**Për ku?**	[pər ku?]
From where?	**Nga ku?**	[ŋa ku?]
When?	**Kur?**	[kur?]
Why? (What for?)	**Pse?**	[psɛ?]
Why? (~ are you crying?)	**Pse?**	[psɛ?]

What for?	**Për çfarë arsye?**	[pər tʃfáre arsýɛ?]
How? (in what way)	**Si?**	[si?]
What? (What kind of ...?)	**Çfarë?**	[tʃfáre?]
Which?	**Cili?**	[tsíli?]

To whom?	**Kujt?**	[kújt?]
About whom?	**Për kë?**	[pər kə?]
About what?	**Për çfarë?**	[pər tʃfáre?]
With whom?	**Me kë?**	[mɛ kə?]

| How many? How much? | **Sa?** | [sa?] |
| Whose? | **Të kujt?** | [tə kujt?] |

4. Prepositions

with (accompanied by)	**me**	[mɛ]
without	**pa**	[pa]
to (indicating direction)	**për në**	[pər nə]
about (talking ~ ...)	**për**	[pər]

before (in time)	**përpara**	[pərpára]
in front of …	**para …**	[pára …]
under (beneath, below)	**nën**	[nən]
above (over)	**mbi**	[mbí]
on (atop)	**mbi**	[mbí]
from (off, out of)	**nga**	[ŋa]
of (made from)	**nga**	[ŋa]
in (e.g., ~ ten minutes)	**për**	[pər]
over (across the top of)	**sipër**	[sípər]

5. Function words. Adverbs. Part 1

Where? (at, in)	**Ku?**	[ku?]
here (adv)	**këtu**	[kətú]
there (adv)	**atje**	[atjé]
somewhere (to be)	**diku**	[dikú]
nowhere (not in any place)	**askund**	[askúnd]
by (near, beside)	**afër**	[áfər]
by the window	**tek dritarja**	[tɛk dritárja]
Where (to)?	**Për ku?**	[pər ku?]
here (e.g., come ~!)	**këtu**	[kətú]
there (e.g., to go ~)	**atje**	[atjé]
from here (adv)	**nga këtu**	[ŋa kətú]
from there (adv)	**nga atje**	[ŋa atjɛ]
close (adv)	**pranë**	[pránə]
far (adv)	**larg**	[larg]
near (e.g., ~ Paris)	**afër**	[áfər]
nearby (adv)	**pranë**	[pránə]
not far (adv)	**jo larg**	[jo lárg]
left (adj)	**majtë**	[májtə]
on the left	**majtas**	[májtas]
to the left	**në të majtë**	[nə tə májtə]
right (adj)	**djathtë**	[djáθtə]
on the right	**djathtas**	[djáθtas]
to the right	**në të djathtë**	[nə tə djáθtə]
in front (adv)	**përballë**	[pərbáłə]
front (as adj)	**i përparmë**	[i pərpármə]
ahead (the kids ran ~)	**përpara**	[pərpára]
behind (adv)	**prapa**	[prápa]
from behind	**nga prapa**	[ŋa prápa]

back (towards the rear)	**pas**	[pas]
middle	**mes** (m)	[mɛs]
in the middle	**në mes**	[nə mɛs]
at the side	**në anë**	[nə anə]
everywhere (adv)	**kudo**	[kúdo]
around (in all directions)	**përreth**	[pəréθ]
from inside	**nga brenda**	[ŋa brénda]
somewhere (to go)	**diku**	[dikú]
straight (directly)	**drejt**	[dréjt]
back (e.g., come ~)	**pas**	[pas]
from anywhere	**nga kudo**	[ŋa kúdo]
from somewhere	**nga diku**	[ŋa dikú]
firstly (adv)	**së pari**	[sə pári]
secondly (adv)	**së dyti**	[sə dýti]
thirdly (adv)	**së treti**	[sə tréti]
suddenly (adv)	**befas**	[béfas]
at first (in the beginning)	**në fillim**	[nə fitím]
for the first time	**për herë të parë**	[pər hérə tə párə]
long before ...	**shumë përpara ...**	[ʃúmə pərpára ...]
anew (over again)	**sërish**	[səríʃ]
for good (adv)	**një herë e mirë**	[ɲə hérə ɛ mírə]
never (adv)	**kurrë**	[kúrə]
again (adv)	**përsëri**	[pərsərí]
now (at present)	**tani**	[táni]
often (adv)	**shpesh**	[ʃpɛʃ]
then (adv)	**atëherë**	[atəhérə]
urgently (quickly)	**urgjent**	[urɲént]
usually (adv)	**zakonisht**	[zakoníʃt]
by the way, ...	**meqë ra fjala, ...**	[mécə ra fjála, ...]
possibly	**ndoshta**	[ndóʃta]
probably (adv)	**mundësisht**	[mundəsíʃt]
maybe (adv)	**mbase**	[mbásɛ]
besides ...	**përveç**	[pərvétʃ]
that's why ...	**ja përse ...**	[ja pərsé ...]
in spite of ...	**pavarësisht se ...**	[pavarəsíʃt sɛ ...]
thanks to ...	**falë ...**	[fálə ...]
what (pron.)	**çfarë**	[tʃfárə]
that (conj.)	**që**	[cə]
something	**diçka**	[ditʃká]
anything (something)	**ndonji gjë**	[ndoɲí ɟə]
nothing	**asgjë**	[asɟé]
who (pron.)	**kush**	[kuʃ]
someone	**dikush**	[dikúʃ]

somebody	dikush	[dikúʃ]
nobody	askush	[askúʃ]
nowhere (a voyage to ~)	askund	[askúnd]
nobody's	i askujt	[i askújt]
somebody's	i dikujt	[i dikújt]

so (I'm ~ glad)	aq	[ác]
also (as well)	gjithashtu	[ɟiθaʃtú]
too (as well)	gjithashtu	[ɟiθaʃtú]

6. Function words. Adverbs. Part 2

Why?	Pse?	[psɛ?]
for some reason	për një arsye	[pər ɲə arsýɛ]
because ...	sepse ...	[sɛpsé ...]
for some purpose	për ndonjë shkak	[pər ndóɲə ʃkak]

and	dhe	[ðɛ]
or	ose	[ósɛ]
but	por	[por]
for (e.g., ~ me)	për	[pər]

too (~ many people)	tepër	[tépər]
only (exclusively)	vetëm	[vétəm]
exactly (adv)	pikërisht	[pikəríʃt]
about (more or less)	rreth	[rɛθ]

approximately (adv)	përafërsisht	[pərafərsíʃt]
approximate (adj)	përafërt	[pəráfərt]
almost (adv)	pothuajse	[poθúajsɛ]
the rest	mbetje (f)	[mbétjɛ]

the other (second)	tjetri	[tjétri]
other (different)	tjetër	[tjétər]
each (adj)	çdo	[tʃdo]
any (no matter which)	çfarëdo	[tʃfarədó]
many (adj)	disa	[disá]
much (adv)	shumë	[ʃúmə]
many people	shumë njerëz	[ʃúmə ɲérəz]
all (everyone)	të gjithë	[tə ɟíθə]

in return for ...	në vend të ...	[nə vénd tə ...]
in exchange (adv)	në shkëmbim të ...	[nə ʃkəmbím tə ...]
by hand (made)	me dorë	[mɛ dórə]
hardly (negative opinion)	vështirë se ...	[vəʃtírə sɛ ...]

probably (adv)	mundësisht	[mundəsíʃt]
on purpose (intentionally)	me qëllim	[mɛ cətím]
by accident (adv)	aksidentalisht	[aksidɛntalíʃt]
very (adv)	shumë	[ʃúmə]

for example (adv)	për shembull	[pər ʃémbuɬ]
between	midis	[midís]
among	rreth	[rɛθ]
so much (such a lot)	kaq shumë	[kác ʃúmə]
especially (adv)	veçanërisht	[vɛtʃanəríʃt]

NUMBERS. MISCELLANEOUS

7. Cardinal numbers. Part 1

0 zero	zero	[zéro]
1 one	një	[ɲə]
2 two	dy	[dy]
3 three	tre	[trɛ]
4 four	katër	[kátər]
5 five	pesë	[pésə]
6 six	gjashtë	[ɟáʃtə]
7 seven	shtatë	[ʃtátə]
8 eight	tetë	[tétə]
9 nine	nëntë	[nəntə]
10 ten	dhjetë	[ðjétə]
11 eleven	njëmbëdhjetë	[ɲəmbəðjétə]
12 twelve	dymbëdhjetë	[dymbəðjétə]
13 thirteen	trembëdhjetë	[trɛmbəðjétə]
14 fourteen	katërmbëdhjetë	[katərmbəðjétə]
15 fifteen	pesëmbëdhjetë	[pɛsəmbəðjétə]
16 sixteen	gjashtëmbëdhjetë	[ɟaʃtəmbəðjétə]
17 seventeen	shtatëmbëdhjetë	[ʃtatəmbəðjétə]
18 eighteen	tetëmbëdhjetë	[tɛtəmbəðjétə]
19 nineteen	nëntëmbëdhjetë	[nəntəmbəðjétə]
20 twenty	njëzet	[ɲəzét]
21 twenty-one	njëzet e një	[ɲəzét ɛ ɲə]
22 twenty-two	njëzet e dy	[ɲəzét ɛ dy]
23 twenty-three	njëzet e tre	[ɲəzét ɛ trɛ]
30 thirty	tridhjetë	[triðjétə]
31 thirty-one	tridhjetë e një	[triðjétə ɛ ɲə]
32 thirty-two	tridhjetë e dy	[triðjétə ɛ dy]
33 thirty-three	tridhjetë e tre	[triðjétə ɛ trɛ]
40 forty	dyzet	[dyzét]
41 forty-one	dyzet e një	[dyzét ɛ ɲə]
42 forty-two	dyzet e dy	[dyzét ɛ dy]
43 forty-three	dyzet e tre	[dyzét ɛ trɛ]
50 fifty	pesëdhjetë	[pɛsəðjétə]
51 fifty-one	pesëdhjetë e një	[pɛsəðjétə ɛ ɲə]
52 fifty-two	pesëdhjetë e dy	[pɛsəðjétə ɛ dy]

53 fifty-three	pesëdhjetë e tre	[pɛsəðjétə ɛ trɛ]
60 sixty	gjashtëdhjetë	[ɟaʃtəðjétə]
61 sixty-one	gjashtëdhjetë e një	[ɟaʃtəðjétə ɛ ɲə]
62 sixty-two	gjashtëdhjetë e dy	[ɟaʃtəðjétə ɛ dý]
63 sixty-three	gjashtëdhjetë e tre	[ɟaʃtəðjétə ɛ tré]
70 seventy	shtatëdhjetë	[ʃtatəðjétə]
71 seventy-one	shtatëdhjetë e një	[ʃtatəðjétə ɛ ɲə]
72 seventy-two	shtatëdhjetë e dy	[ʃtatəðjétə ɛ dy]
73 seventy-three	shtatëdhjetë e tre	[ʃtatəðjétə ɛ trɛ]
80 eighty	tetëdhjetë	[tɛtəðjétə]
81 eighty-one	tetëdhjetë e një	[tɛtəðjétə ɛ ɲə]
82 eighty-two	tetëdhjetë e dy	[tɛtəðjétə ɛ dy]
83 eighty-three	tetëdhjetë e tre	[tɛtəðjétə ɛ trɛ]
90 ninety	nëntëdhjetë	[nəntəðjétə]
91 ninety-one	nëntëdhjetë e një	[nəntəðjétə ɛ ɲə]
92 ninety-two	nëntëdhjetë e dy	[nəntəðjétə ɛ dy]
93 ninety-three	nëntëdhjetë e tre	[nəntəðjétə ɛ trɛ]

8. Cardinal numbers. Part 2

100 one hundred	njëqind	[ɲəcínd]
200 two hundred	dyqind	[dycínd]
300 three hundred	treqind	[trɛcínd]
400 four hundred	katërqind	[katərcínd]
500 five hundred	pesëqind	[pɛsəcínd]
600 six hundred	gjashtëqind	[ɟaʃtecínd]
700 seven hundred	shtatëqind	[ʃtatecínd]
800 eight hundred	tetëqind	[tɛtecínd]
900 nine hundred	nëntëqind	[nəntecínd]
1000 one thousand	një mijë	[ɲə míjə]
2000 two thousand	dy mijë	[dy míjə]
3000 three thousand	tre mijë	[trɛ míjə]
10000 ten thousand	dhjetë mijë	[ðjétə míjə]
one hundred thousand	njëqind mijë	[ɲəcínd míjə]
million	milion (m)	[milión]
billion	miliardë (f)	[miliárdə]

9. Ordinal numbers

first (adj)	i pari	[i pári]
second (adj)	i dyti	[i dýti]
third (adj)	i treti	[i tréti]
fourth (adj)	i katërti	[i kátərti]

fifth (adj)	i pesti	[i pésti]
sixth (adj)	i gjashti	[i ɟáʃti]
seventh (adj)	i shtati	[i ʃtáti]
eighth (adj)	i teti	[i téti]
ninth (adj)	i nënti	[i nénti]
tenth (adj)	i dhjeti	[i ðjéti]

COLOURS. UNITS OF MEASUREMENT

10. Colors

color	ngjyrë (f)	[ɲýrə]
shade (tint)	nuancë (f)	[nuántsə]
hue	tonalitet (m)	[tonalitét]
rainbow	ylber (m)	[ylbéɾ]
white (adj)	e bardhë	[ɛ báɾðə]
black (adj)	e zezë	[ɛ zézə]
gray (adj)	gri	[gri]
green (adj)	jeshile	[jɛʃílɛ]
yellow (adj)	e verdhë	[ɛ véɾðə]
red (adj)	e kuqe	[ɛ kúcɛ]
blue (adj)	blu	[blu]
light blue (adj)	bojëqielli	[bojəciéɫi]
pink (adj)	rozë	[rózə]
orange (adj)	portokalli	[portokáɫi]
violet (adj)	bojëvjollcë	[bojəvjóɫtsə]
brown (adj)	kafe	[káfɛ]
golden (adj)	e artë	[ɛ áɾtə]
silvery (adj)	e argjendtë	[ɛ aɾɟéndtə]
beige (adj)	bezhë	[béʒə]
cream (adj)	krem	[krɛm]
turquoise (adj)	e bruztë	[ɛ brúztə]
cherry red (adj)	qershi	[cɛɾʃí]
lilac (adj)	jargavan	[jargaván]
crimson (adj)	e kuqe e thellë	[ɛ kúcɛ ɛ θéɫə]
light (adj)	e hapur	[ɛ hápuɾ]
dark (adj)	e errët	[ɛ éɾət]
bright, vivid (adj)	e ndritshme	[ɛ ndrítʃmɛ]
colored (pencils)	e ngjyrosur	[ɛ ɲyrósuɾ]
color (e.g., ~ film)	ngjyrë	[ɲýrə]
black-and-white (adj)	bardhë e zi	[báɾðə ɛ zi]
plain (one-colored)	njëngjyrëshe	[nənɟýrəʃɛ]
multicolored (adj)	shumëngjyrëshe	[ʃumənɟýrəʃɛ]

11. Units of measurement

weight	peshë (f)	[péʃə]
length	gjatësi (f)	[ɟatəsí]
width	gjerësi (f)	[ɟɛrəsí]
height	lartësi (f)	[lartəsí]
depth	thellësi (f)	[θɛɫəsí]
volume	vëllim (m)	[vəɫím]
area	sipërfaqe (f)	[sipərfácɛ]

gram	gram (m)	[gram]
milligram	miligram (m)	[miligrám]
kilogram	kilogram (m)	[kilográm]
ton	ton (m)	[ton]
pound	paund (m)	[páund]
ounce	ons (m)	[ons]

meter	metër (m)	[métər]
millimeter	milimetër (m)	[milimétər]
centimeter	centimetër (m)	[tsɛntimétər]
kilometer	kilometër (m)	[kilométər]
mile	milje (f)	[míljɛ]

inch	inç (m)	[intʃ]
foot	këmbë (f)	[kémbə]
yard	jard (m)	[járd]

square meter	metër katror (m)	[métər katrór]
hectare	hektar (m)	[hɛktár]

liter	litër (m)	[lítər]
degree	gradë (f)	[grádə]
volt	volt (m)	[volt]
ampere	amper (m)	[ampér]
horsepower	kuaj-fuqi (f)	[kúaj-fucí]

quantity	sasi (f)	[sasí]
a little bit of …	pak …	[pak …]
half	gjysmë (f)	[ɟýsmə]

dozen	dyzinë (f)	[dyzínə]
piece (item)	copë (f)	[tsópə]

size	madhësi (f)	[maðəsí]
scale (map ~)	shkallë (f)	[ʃkáɫə]

minimal (adj)	minimale	[minimálɛ]
the smallest (adj)	më i vogli	[mə i vógli]
medium (adj)	i mesëm	[i mésəm]
maximal (adj)	maksimale	[maksimálɛ]
the largest (adj)	më i madhi	[mə i máði]

12. Containers

canning jar (glass ~)	**kavanoz** (m)	[kavanóz]
can	**kanoçe** (f)	[kanótʃɛ]
bucket	**kovë** (f)	[kóvə]
barrel	**fuçi** (f)	[futʃí]
wash basin (e.g., plastic ~)	**legen** (m)	[lɛgén]
tank (100L water ~)	**tank** (m)	[tank]
hip flask	**faqore** (f)	[facórɛ]
jerrycan	**bidon** (m)	[bidón]
tank (e.g., tank car)	**cisternë** (f)	[tsistérnə]
mug	**tas** (m)	[tas]
cup (of coffee, etc.)	**filxhan** (m)	[fildʒán]
saucer	**pjatë filxhani** (f)	[pjátə fildʒáni]
glass (tumbler)	**gotë** (f)	[gótə]
wine glass	**gotë vere** (f)	[gótə vérɛ]
stock pot (soup pot)	**tenxhere** (f)	[tɛndʒérɛ]
bottle (~ of wine)	**shishe** (f)	[ʃíʃɛ]
neck (of the bottle, etc.)	**grykë**	[grýkə]
carafe (decanter)	**brokë** (f)	[brókə]
pitcher	**shtambë** (f)	[ʃtámbə]
vessel (container)	**enë** (f)	[énə]
pot (crock, stoneware ~)	**enë** (f)	[énə]
vase	**vazo** (f)	[vázo]
flacon, bottle (perfume ~)	**shishe** (f)	[ʃíʃɛ]
vial, small bottle	**shishkë** (f)	[ʃíʃkə]
tube (of toothpaste)	**tubet** (f)	[tubét]
sack (bag)	**thes** (m)	[θɛs]
bag (paper ~, plastic ~)	**qese** (f)	[césɛ]
pack (of cigarettes, etc.)	**paketë** (f)	[pakétə]
box (e.g., shoebox)	**kuti** (f)	[kutí]
crate	**arkë** (f)	[árkə]
basket	**shportë** (f)	[ʃpórtə]

MAIN VERBS

13. The most important verbs. Part 1

to advise (vt)	këshilloj	[kəʃiɫój]
to agree (say yes)	bie dakord	[bíɛ dakórd]
to answer (vi, vt)	përgjigjem	[pərɟíɟɛm]
to apologize (vi)	kërkoj falje	[kərkój fáljɛ]
to arrive (vi)	arrij	[aríj]
to ask (~ oneself)	pyes	[pýɛs]
to ask (~ sb to do sth)	pyes	[pýɛs]
to be (vi)	jam	[jam]
to be afraid	kam frikë	[kam fríkə]
to be hungry	kam uri	[kam urí]
to be interested in ...	interesohem ...	[intɛrɛsóhɛm ...]
to be needed	nevojitet	[nɛvojítɛt]
to be surprised	çuditem	[tʃudítɛm]
to be thirsty	kam etje	[kam étjɛ]
to begin (vt)	filloj	[fiɫój]
to belong to ...	përkas ...	[pərkás ...]
to boast (vi)	mburrem	[mbúrɛm]
to break (split into pieces)	ndahem	[ndáhɛm]
to call (~ for help)	thërras	[θərás]
can (v aux)	mund	[mund]
to catch (vt)	kap	[kap]
to change (vt)	ndryshoj	[ndryʃój]
to choose (select)	zgjedh	[ʒɟɛð]
to come down (the stairs)	zbres	[zbrɛs]
to compare (vt)	krahasoj	[krahasój]
to complain (vi, vt)	ankohem	[ankóhɛm]
to confuse (mix up)	ngatërroj	[ŋatərój]
to continue (vt)	vazhdoj	[vaʒdój]
to control (vt)	kontrolloj	[kontroɫój]
to cook (dinner)	gatuaj	[gatúaj]
to cost (vt)	kushton	[kuʃtón]
to count (add up)	numëroj	[numərój]
to count on ...	mbështetem ...	[mbəʃtétɛm ...]
to create (vt)	krijoj	[krijój]
to cry (weep)	qaj	[caj]

14. The most important verbs. Part 2

to deceive (vi, vt)	mashtroj	[maʃtrój]
to decorate (tree, street)	zbukuroj	[zbukurój]
to defend (a country, etc.)	mbroj	[mbrój]
to demand (request firmly)	kërkoj	[kərkój]
to dig (vt)	gërmoj	[gərmój]

to discuss (vt)	diskutoj	[diskutój]
to do (vt)	bëj	[bəj]
to doubt (have doubts)	dyshoj	[dyʃój]
to drop (let fall)	lëshoj	[ləʃój]
to enter (room, house, etc.)	hyj	[hyj]

to excuse (forgive)	fal	[fal]
to exist (vi)	ekzistoj	[ɛkzistój]
to expect (foresee)	parashikoj	[paraʃikój]

to explain (vt)	shpjegoj	[ʃpjɛgój]
to fall (vi)	bie	[bíɛ]

to find (vt)	gjej	[ɟéj]
to finish (vt)	përfundoj	[pərfundój]
to fly (vi)	fluturoj	[fluturój]

to follow ... (come after)	ndjek ...	[ndjék ...]
to forget (vi, vt)	harroj	[harój]

to forgive (vt)	fal	[fal]
to give (vt)	jap	[jap]

to give a hint	aludoj	[aludój]
to go (on foot)	ec në këmbë	[ɛts nə kémbə]

to go for a swim	notoj	[notój]
to go out (for dinner, etc.)	dal	[dal]
to guess (the answer)	hamendësoj	[hamɛndəsój]

to have (vt)	kam	[kam]
to have breakfast	ha mëngjes	[ha mənɟés]
to have dinner	ha darkë	[ha dárkə]

to have lunch	ha drekë	[ha drékə]
to hear (vt)	dëgjoj	[dəɟój]

to help (vt)	ndihmoj	[ndihmój]
to hide (vt)	fsheh	[fʃéh]
to hope (vi, vt)	shpresoj	[ʃprɛsój]
to hunt (vi, vt)	dal për gjah	[dál pər ɟáh]
to hurry (vi)	nxitoj	[ndzitój]

15. The most important verbs. Part 3

to inform (vt)	informoj	[informój]
to insist (vi, vt)	këmbëngul	[kəmbəŋúl]
to insult (vt)	fyej	[fýɛj]
to invite (vt)	ftoj	[ftoj]
to joke (vi)	bëj shaka	[bəj ʃaká]
to keep (vt)	mbaj	[mbáj]
to keep silent, to hush	hesht	[hɛʃt]
to kill (vt)	vras	[vras]
to know (sb)	njoh	[ɲóh]
to know (sth)	di	[di]
to laugh (vi)	qesh	[cɛʃ]
to liberate (city, etc.)	çliroj	[tʃlirój]
to like (I like ...)	pëlqej	[pəlcéj]
to look for ... (search)	kërkoj ...	[kərkój ...]
to love (sb)	dashuroj	[daʃurój]
to make a mistake	gaboj	[gabój]
to manage, to run	drejtoj	[drɛjtój]
to mean (signify)	nënkuptoj	[nənkuptój]
to mention (talk about)	përmend	[pərménd]
to miss (school, etc.)	humbas	[humbás]
to notice (see)	vërej	[vəréj]
to object (vi, vt)	kundërshtoj	[kundərʃtój]
to observe (see)	vëzhgoj	[vəʒgój]
to open (vt)	hap	[hap]
to order (meal, etc.)	porosis	[porosís]
to order (mil.)	urdhëroj	[urðərój]
to own (possess)	zotëroj	[zotərój]
to participate (vi)	marr pjesë	[mar pjésə]
to pay (vi, vt)	paguaj	[pagúaj]
to permit (vt)	lejoj	[lɛjój]
to plan (vt)	planifikoj	[planifikój]
to play (children)	luaj	[lúaj]
to pray (vi, vt)	lutem	[lútɛm]
to prefer (vt)	preferoj	[prɛfɛrój]
to promise (vt)	premtoj	[prɛmtój]
to pronounce (vt)	shqiptoj	[ʃciptój]
to propose (vt)	propozoj	[propozój]
to punish (vt)	ndëshkoj	[ndəʃkój]

16. The most important verbs. Part 4

to read (vi, vt)	lexoj	[lɛdzój]
to recommend (vt)	rekomandoj	[rɛkomandój]

to refuse (vi, vt)	**refuzoj**	[rɛfuzój]
to regret (be sorry)	**pendohem**	[pɛndóhɛm]
to rent (sth from sb)	**marr me qira**	[mar mɛ cirá]
to repeat (say again)	**përsëris**	[pərsərís]
to reserve, to book	**rezervoj**	[rɛzɛrvój]
to run (vi)	**vrapoj**	[vrapój]
to save (rescue)	**shpëtoj**	[ʃpətój]
to say (~ thank you)	**them**	[θɛm]
to scold (vt)	**qortoj**	[cortój]
to see (vt)	**shikoj**	[ʃikój]
to sell (vt)	**shes**	[ʃɛs]
to send (vt)	**dërgoj**	[dərgój]
to shoot (vi)	**qëlloj**	[cəɫój]
to shout (vi)	**bërtas**	[bərtás]
to show (vt)	**tregoj**	[trɛgój]
to sign (document)	**nënshkruaj**	[nənʃkrúaj]
to sit down (vi)	**ulem**	[úlɛm]
to smile (vi)	**buzëqesh**	[buzəcéʃ]
to speak (vi, vt)	**flas**	[flas]
to steal (money, etc.)	**vjedh**	[vjɛð]
to stop (for pause, etc.)	**ndaloj**	[ndalój]
to stop (please ~ calling me)	**ndaloj**	[ndalój]
to study (vt)	**studioj**	[studiój]
to swim (vi)	**notoj**	[notój]
to take (vt)	**marr**	[mar]
to think (vi, vt)	**mendoj**	[mɛndój]
to threaten (vt)	**kërcënoj**	[kərtsənój]
to touch (with hands)	**prek**	[prɛk]
to translate (vt)	**përkthej**	[pərkθéj]
to trust (vt)	**besoj**	[bɛsój]
to try (attempt)	**përpiqem**	[pərpícɛm]
to turn (e.g., ~ left)	**kthej**	[kθɛj]
to underestimate (vt)	**nënvlerësoj**	[nənvlɛrəsój]
to understand (vt)	**kuptoj**	[kuptój]
to unite (vt)	**bashkoj**	[baʃkój]
to wait (vt)	**pres**	[prɛs]
to want (wish, desire)	**dëshiroj**	[dəʃirój]
to warn (vt)	**paralajmëroj**	[paralajmərój]
to work (vi)	**punoj**	[punój]
to write (vt)	**shkruaj**	[ʃkrúaj]
to write down	**mbaj shënim**	[mbáj ʃəním]

TIME. CALENDAR

17. Weekdays

Monday	**E hënë** (f)	[ɛ hénə]
Tuesday	**E martë** (f)	[ɛ mártə]
Wednesday	**E mërkurë** (f)	[ɛ mərkúrə]
Thursday	**E enjte** (f)	[ɛ éɲtɛ]
Friday	**E premte** (f)	[ɛ prémtɛ]
Saturday	**E shtunë** (f)	[ɛ ʃtúnə]
Sunday	**E dielë** (f)	[ɛ díɛlə]
today (adv)	**sot**	[sot]
tomorrow (adv)	**nesër**	[nésər]
the day after tomorrow	**pasnesër**	[pasnésər]
yesterday (adv)	**dje**	[djé]
the day before yesterday	**pardje**	[pardjé]
day	**ditë** (f)	[dítə]
working day	**ditë pune** (f)	[dítə púnɛ]
public holiday	**festë kombëtare** (f)	[féstə kombətárɛ]
day off	**ditë pushim** (m)	[dítə puʃím]
weekend	**fundjavë** (f)	[fundjávə]
all day long	**gjithë ditën**	[ɟíθə dítən]
the next day (adv)	**ditën pasardhëse**	[dítən pasárðəsɛ]
two days ago	**dy ditë më parë**	[dy dítə mə párə]
the day before	**një ditë më parë**	[ɲə dítə mə párə]
daily (adj)	**ditor**	[ditór]
every day (adv)	**çdo ditë**	[tʃdo dítə]
week	**javë** (f)	[jávə]
last week (adv)	**javën e kaluar**	[jávən ɛ kalúar]
next week (adv)	**javën e ardhshme**	[jávən ɛ árðʃmɛ]
weekly (adj)	**javor**	[javór]
every week (adv)	**çdo javë**	[tʃdo jávə]
twice a week	**dy herë në javë**	[dy hérə nə jávə]
every Tuesday	**çdo të martë**	[tʃdo tə mártə]

18. Hours. Day and night

morning	**mëngjes** (m)	[məɲɟés]
in the morning	**në mëngjes**	[nə məɲɟés]
noon, midday	**mesditë** (f)	[mɛsdítə]

in the afternoon	**pasdite**	[pasdítɛ]
evening	**mbrëmje** (f)	[mbrémjɛ]
in the evening	**në mbrëmje**	[nə mbrémjɛ]
night	**natë** (f)	[nátə]
at night	**natën**	[nátən]
midnight	**mesnatë** (f)	[mɛsnátə]

second	**sekondë** (f)	[sɛkóndə]
minute	**minutë** (f)	[minútə]
hour	**orë** (f)	[órə]
half an hour	**gjysmë ore** (f)	[ɟýsmə órɛ]
a quarter-hour	**çerek ore** (m)	[tʃɛrék órɛ]
fifteen minutes	**pesëmbëdhjetë minuta**	[pɛsəmbəðjétə minúta]
24 hours	**24 orë**	[ɲəzét ɛ kátər órə]

sunrise	**agim** (m)	[agím]
dawn	**agim** (m)	[agím]
early morning	**mëngjes herët** (m)	[mənɟés hérət]
sunset	**perëndim dielli** (m)	[pɛrəndím diéłi]

early in the morning	**herët në mëngjes**	[hérət nə mənɟés]
this morning	**sot në mëngjes**	[sot nə mənɟés]
tomorrow morning	**nesër në mëngjes**	[nésər nə mənɟés]

this afternoon	**sot pasdite**	[sot pasdítɛ]
in the afternoon	**pasdite**	[pasdítɛ]
tomorrow afternoon	**nesër pasdite**	[nésər pasdítɛ]

| tonight (this evening) | **sonte në mbrëmje** | [sóntɛ nə mbrəmjɛ] |
| tomorrow night | **nesër në mbrëmje** | [nésər nə mbrémjɛ] |

at 3 o'clock sharp	**në orën 3 fiks**	[nə órən trɛ fiks]
about 4 o'clock	**rreth orës 4**	[rɛθ órəs kátər]
by 12 o'clock	**deri në orën 12**	[déri nə órən dymbəðjétə]

in 20 minutes	**për 20 minuta**	[pər ɲəzét minúta]
in an hour	**për një orë**	[pər ɲə órə]
on time (adv)	**në orar**	[nə orár]

a quarter to ...	**çerek ...**	[tʃɛrék ...]
within an hour	**brenda një ore**	[brénda ɲə órɛ]
every 15 minutes	**çdo 15 minuta**	[tʃdo pɛsəmbəðjétə minúta]
round the clock	**gjithë ditën**	[ɟíθə dítən]

19. Months. Seasons

January	**Janar** (m)	[janár]
February	**Shkurt** (m)	[ʃkurt]
March	**Mars** (m)	[mars]
April	**Prill** (m)	[priɬ]

May	**Maj** (m)	[maj]
June	**Qershor** (m)	[cɛrʃór]
July	**Korrik** (m)	[korík]
August	**Gusht** (m)	[guʃt]
September	**Shtator** (m)	[ʃtatór]
October	**Tetor** (m)	[tɛtór]
November	**Nëntor** (m)	[nəntór]
December	**Dhjetor** (m)	[ðjɛtór]
spring	**pranverë** (f)	[pranvérə]
in spring	**në pranverë**	[nə pranvérə]
spring (as adj)	**pranveror**	[pranvɛrór]
summer	**verë** (f)	[vérə]
in summer	**në verë**	[nə vérə]
summer (as adj)	**veror**	[vɛrór]
fall	**vjeshtë** (f)	[vjéʃtə]
in fall	**në vjeshtë**	[nə vjéʃtə]
fall (as adj)	**vjeshtor**	[vjéʃtor]
winter	**dimër** (m)	[dímər]
in winter	**në dimër**	[nə dímər]
winter (as adj)	**dimëror**	[dimərór]
month	**muaj** (m)	[múaj]
this month	**këtë muaj**	[kətə múaj]
next month	**muajin tjetër**	[múajin tjétər]
last month	**muajin e kaluar**	[múajin ɛ kalúar]
a month ago	**para një muaji**	[pára ɲə múaji]
in a month (a month later)	**pas një muaji**	[pas ɲə múaji]
in 2 months (2 months later)	**pas dy muajsh**	[pas dy múajʃ]
the whole month	**gjithë muajin**	[ɟíθə múajin]
all month long	**gjatë gjithë muajit**	[ɟátə ɟíθə múajit]
monthly (~ magazine)	**mujor**	[mujór]
monthly (adv)	**mujor**	[mujór]
every month	**çdo muaj**	[tʃdo múaj]
twice a month	**dy herë në muaj**	[dy hérə nə múaj]
year	**vit** (m)	[vit]
this year	**këtë vit**	[kətə vít]
next year	**vitin tjetër**	[vítin tjétər]
last year	**vitin e kaluar**	[vítin ɛ kalúar]
a year ago	**para një viti**	[pára ɲə víti]
in a year	**për një vit**	[pər ɲə vit]
in two years	**për dy vite**	[pər dy vítɛ]
the whole year	**gjithë vitin**	[ɟíθə vítin]

all year long	gjatë gjithë vitit	[ɟátə ɟíθə vítit]
every year	çdo vit	[tʃdo vít]
annual (adj)	vjetor	[vjɛtór]
annually (adv)	çdo vit	[tʃdo vít]
4 times a year	4 herë në vit	[kátər hérə nə vit]

date (e.g., today's ~)	datë (f)	[dátə]
date (e.g., ~ of birth)	data (f)	[dáta]
calendar	kalendar (m)	[kalɛndár]

half a year	gjysmë viti	[ɟýsmə víti]
six months	gjashtë muaj	[ɟáʃtə múaj]
season (summer, etc.)	stinë (f)	[stínə]
century	shekull (m)	[ʃékuɫ]

TRAVEL. HOTEL

20. Trip. Travel

tourism, travel	**turizëm** (m)	[turízəm]
tourist	**turist** (m)	[turíst]
trip, voyage	**udhëtim** (m)	[uðətím]
adventure	**aventurë** (f)	[avɛntúrə]
trip, journey	**udhëtim** (m)	[uðətím]
vacation	**pushim** (m)	[puʃím]
to be on vacation	**jam me pushime**	[jam mɛ puʃímɛ]
rest	**pushim** (m)	[puʃím]
train	**tren** (m)	[trɛn]
by train	**me tren**	[mɛ trén]
airplane	**avion** (m)	[avión]
by airplane	**me avion**	[mɛ avión]
by car	**me makinë**	[mɛ makínə]
by ship	**me anije**	[mɛ aníjɛ]
luggage	**bagazh** (m)	[bagáʒ]
suitcase	**valixhe** (f)	[valídʒɛ]
luggage cart	**karrocë bagazhesh** (f)	[karótsə bagáʒɛʃ]
passport	**pasaportë** (f)	[pasapórtə]
visa	**vizë** (f)	[vízə]
ticket	**biletë** (f)	[bilétə]
air ticket	**biletë avioni** (f)	[bilétə avióni]
guidebook	**guidë turistike** (f)	[guídə turistíkɛ]
map (tourist ~)	**hartë** (f)	[hártə]
area (rural ~)	**zonë** (f)	[zónə]
place, site	**vend** (m)	[vɛnd]
exotica (n)	**ekzotikë** (f)	[ɛkzotíkə]
exotic (adj)	**ekzotik**	[ɛkzotík]
amazing (adj)	**mahnitëse**	[mahnítəsɛ]
group	**grup** (m)	[grup]
excursion, sightseeing tour	**ekskursion** (m)	[ɛkskursión]
guide (person)	**udhërrëfyes** (m)	[uðərəfýɛs]

21. Hotel

hotel, inn	**hotel** (m)	[hotél]
motel	**motel** (m)	[motél]
three-star (~ hotel)	**me tre yje**	[mɛ trɛ ýjɛ]
five-star	**me pesë yje**	[mɛ pésə ýjɛ]
to stay (in a hotel, etc.)	**qëndroj**	[cəndrój]
room	**dhomë** (f)	[ðómə]
single room	**dhomë teke** (f)	[ðómə tékɛ]
double room	**dhomë dyshe** (f)	[ðómə dýʃɛ]
to book a room	**rezervoj një dhomë**	[rɛzɛrvój ɲə ðómə]
half board	**gjysmë-pension** (m)	[ɟýsmə-pɛnsión]
full board	**pension i plotë** (m)	[pɛnsión i plótə]
with bath	**me banjo**	[mɛ báɲo]
with shower	**me dush**	[mɛ dúʃ]
satellite television	**televizor satelitor** (m)	[tɛlɛvizór satɛlitór]
air-conditioner	**kondicioner** (m)	[konditsionér]
towel	**peshqir** (m)	[pɛʃcír]
key	**çelës** (m)	[tʃéləs]
administrator	**administrator** (m)	[administratór]
chambermaid	**pastruese** (f)	[pastrúɛsɛ]
porter, bellboy	**portier** (m)	[portiér]
doorman	**portier** (m)	[portiér]
restaurant	**restorant** (m)	[rɛstoránt]
pub, bar	**pab** (m), **pijetore** (f)	[pab], [pijɛtórɛ]
breakfast	**mëngjes** (m)	[mənɟés]
dinner	**darkë** (f)	[dárkə]
buffet	**bufe** (f)	[bufé]
lobby	**holl** (m)	[hoɫ]
elevator	**ashensor** (m)	[aʃɛnsór]
DO NOT DISTURB	**MOS SHQETËSONI**	[mos ʃcɛtəsóni]
NO SMOKING	**NDALOHET DUHANI**	[ndalóhɛt duháni]

22. Sightseeing

monument	**monument** (m)	[monumént]
fortress	**kala** (f)	[kalá]
palace	**pallat** (m)	[paɫát]
castle	**kështjellë** (f)	[kəʃtjéɫə]
tower	**kullë** (f)	[kúɫə]
mausoleum	**mauzoleum** (m)	[mauzolɛúm]

architecture	**arkitekturë** (f)	[arkitɛktúrə]
medieval (adj)	**mesjetare**	[mɛsjɛtárɛ]
ancient (adj)	**e lashtë**	[ɛ láʃtə]
national (adj)	**kombëtare**	[kombətárɛ]
famous (monument, etc.)	**i famshëm**	[i fámʃəm]

tourist	**turist** (m)	[turíst]
guide (person)	**udhërrëfyes** (m)	[uðərəfýɛs]
excursion, sightseeing tour	**ekskursion** (m)	[ɛkskursión]
to show (vt)	**tregoj**	[trɛgój]
to tell (vt)	**dëftoj**	[dəftój]

to find (vt)	**gjej**	[ɟéj]
to get lost (lose one's way)	**humbas**	[humbás]
map (e.g., subway ~)	**hartë** (f)	[hártə]
map (e.g., city ~)	**hartë** (f)	[hártə]

souvenir, gift	**suvenir** (m)	[suvɛnír]
gift shop	**dyqan dhuratash** (m)	[dycán ðurátaʃ]
to take pictures	**bëj foto**	[bəj fóto]
to have one's picture taken	**bëj fotografi**	[bəj fotografí]

TRANSPORTATION

23. Airport

airport	**aeroport** (m)	[aɛropórt]
airplane	**avion** (m)	[avión]
airline	**kompani ajrore** (f)	[kompaní ajrórɛ]
air traffic controller	**kontroll i trafikut ajror** (m)	[kontróɫ i trafíkut ajrór]
departure	**nisje** (f)	[nísjɛ]
arrival	**arritje** (f)	[arítjɛ]
to arrive (by plane)	**arrij me avion**	[aríj mɛ avión]
departure time	**nisja** (f)	[nísja]
arrival time	**arritja** (f)	[arítja]
to be delayed	**vonesë**	[vonésə]
flight delay	**vonesë avioni** (f)	[vonésə avióni]
information board	**ekrani i informacioneve** (m)	[ɛkráni i informatsiónɛvɛ]
information	**informacion** (m)	[informatsión]
to announce (vt)	**njoftoj**	[ɲoftój]
flight (e.g., next ~)	**fluturim** (m)	[fluturím]
customs	**doganë** (f)	[dogánə]
customs officer	**doganier** (m)	[doganiér]
customs declaration	**deklarim doganor** (m)	[dɛklarím doganór]
to fill out (vt)	**plotësoj**	[plotəsój]
to fill out the declaration	**plotësoj deklaratën**	[plotəsój dɛklarátən]
passport control	**kontroll pasaportash** (m)	[kontróɫ pasapórtaʃ]
luggage	**bagazh** (m)	[bagáʒ]
hand luggage	**bagazh dore** (m)	[bagáʒ dórɛ]
luggage cart	**karrocë bagazhesh** (f)	[karótsə bagáʒɛʃ]
landing	**aterrim** (m)	[atɛrím]
landing strip	**pistë aterrimi** (f)	[pístə atɛrími]
to land (vi)	**aterroj**	[atɛrój]
airstair (passenger stair)	**shkallë avioni** (f)	[ʃkáɫə avióni]
check-in	**regjistrim** (m)	[rɛɟistrím]
check-in counter	**sportel regjistrimi** (m)	[sportél rɛɟistrími]
to check-in (vi)	**regjistrohem**	[rɛɟistróhɛm]
boarding pass	**biletë e hyrjes** (f)	[bilétə ɛ hýrjɛs]

departure gate	porta e nisjes (f)	[pórta ε nísjεs]
transit	transit (m)	[transít]
to wait (vt)	pres	[prεs]
departure lounge	salla e nisjes (f)	[sáła ε nísjεs]
to see off	përcjell	[pərtsjéł]
to say goodbye	përshëndetem	[pərʃəndétεm]

24. Airplane

airplane	avion (m)	[avión]
air ticket	biletë avioni (f)	[bilétə avióni]
airline	kompani ajrore (f)	[kompaní ajrórε]
airport	aeroport (m)	[aεropórt]
supersonic (adj)	supersonik	[supεrsoník]

captain	kapiten (m)	[kapitén]
crew	ekip (m)	[εkíp]
pilot	pilot (m)	[pilót]
flight attendant (fem.)	stjuardesë (f)	[stjuardésə]
navigator	navigues (m)	[navigúεs]

wings	krahë (pl)	[kráhə]
tail	bisht (m)	[biʃt]
cockpit	kabinë (f)	[kabínə]
engine	motor (m)	[motór]
undercarriage (landing gear)	karrel (m)	[karél]
turbine	turbinë (f)	[turbínə]

propeller	helikë (f)	[hεlíkə]
black box	kuti e zezë (f)	[kutí ε zézə]
yoke (control column)	timon (m)	[timón]
fuel	karburant (m)	[karburánt]

safety card	udhëzime sigurie (pl)	[uðəzímε siguríε]
oxygen mask	maskë oksigjeni (f)	[máskə oksiɟéni]
uniform	uniformë (f)	[unifórmə]
life vest	jelek shpëtimi (m)	[jεlék ʃpətími]
parachute	parashutë (f)	[paraʃútə]

takeoff	ngritje (f)	[ŋrítjε]
to take off (vi)	fluturon	[fluturón]
runway	pista e fluturimit (f)	[písta ε fluturímit]

visibility	shikueshmëri (f)	[ʃikuεʃmərí]
flight (act of flying)	fluturim (m)	[fluturím]
altitude	lartësi (f)	[lartəsí]
air pocket	xhep ajri (m)	[dʒεp ájri]
seat	karrige (f)	[karígε]
headphones	kufje (f)	[kúfjε]

folding tray (tray table)	**tabaka** (f)	[tabaká]
airplane window	**dritare avioni** (f)	[dritárɛ avióni]
aisle	**korridor** (m)	[koridór]

25. Train

train	**tren** (m)	[trɛn]
commuter train	**tren elektrik** (m)	[trɛn ɛlɛktrík]
express train	**tren ekspres** (m)	[trɛn ɛksprés]
diesel locomotive	**lokomotivë me naftë** (f)	[lokomótivə mɛ náftə]
steam locomotive	**lokomotivë me avull** (f)	[lokomótivə mɛ ávuɫ]

| passenger car | **vagon** (m) | [vagón] |
| dining car | **vagon restorant** (m) | [vagón rɛstoránt] |

rails	**shina** (pl)	[ʃína]
railroad	**hekurudhë** (f)	[hɛkurúðə]
railway tie	**traversë** (f)	[travérsə]

platform (railway ~)	**platformë** (f)	[platfórmə]
track (~ 1, 2, etc.)	**binar** (m)	[binár]
semaphore	**semafor** (m)	[sɛmafór]
station	**stacion** (m)	[statsión]

engineer (train driver)	**makinist** (m)	[makiníst]
porter (of luggage)	**portier** (m)	[portiér]
car attendant	**konduktor** (m)	[konduktór]
passenger	**pasagjer** (m)	[pasaɟér]
conductor (ticket inspector)	**konduktor** (m)	[konduktór]

| corridor (in train) | **korridor** (m) | [koridór] |
| emergency brake | **frena urgjence** (f) | [fréna urɟéntsɛ] |

compartment	**ndarje** (f)	[ndárjɛ]
berth	**kat** (m)	[kat]
upper berth	**kati i sipërm** (m)	[káti i sípərm]
lower berth	**kati i poshtëm** (m)	[káti i póʃtəm]
bed linen, bedding	**shtroje shtrati** (pl)	[ʃtrójɛ ʃtráti]

ticket	**biletë** (f)	[bilétə]
schedule	**orar** (m)	[orár]
information display	**tabelë e informatave** (f)	[tabélə ɛ informátavɛ]

to leave, to depart	**niset**	[nísɛt]
departure (of train)	**nisje** (f)	[nísjɛ]
to arrive (ab. train)	**arrij**	[aríj]
arrival	**arritje** (f)	[arítjɛ]
to arrive by train	**arrij me tren**	[aríj mɛ trɛn]
to get on the train	**hip në tren**	[hip nə trén]

to get off the train	**zbres nga treni**	[zbrɛs ŋa tréni]
train wreck	**aksident hekurudhor** (m)	[aksidént hɛkuruðór]
to derail (vi)	**del nga shinat**	[dɛl ŋa ʃínat]
steam locomotive	**lokomotivë me avull** (f)	[lokomótivə mɛ ávuł]
stoker, fireman	**mbikëqyrës i zjarrit** (m)	[mbikəcýrəs i zjárit]
firebox	**furrë** (f)	[fúrə]
coal	**qymyr** (m)	[cymýr]

26. Ship

ship	**anije** (f)	[aníjɛ]
vessel	**mjet lundrues** (m)	[mjét lundrúɛs]
steamship	**anije me avull** (f)	[aníjɛ mɛ ávuł]
riverboat	**anije lumi** (f)	[aníjɛ lúmi]
cruise ship	**krocierë** (f)	[krotsiérə]
cruiser	**anije luftarake** (f)	[aníjɛ luftarákɛ]
yacht	**jaht** (m)	[jáht]
tugboat	**anije rimorkiuese** (f)	[aníjɛ rimorkiúɛsɛ]
barge	**anije transportuese** (f)	[aníjɛ transportúɛsɛ]
ferry	**traget** (m)	[tragét]
sailing ship	**anije me vela** (f)	[aníjɛ mɛ véla]
brigantine	**brigantinë** (f)	[brigantínə]
ice breaker	**akullthyese** (f)	[akułθýɛsɛ]
submarine	**nëndetëse** (f)	[nəndétəsɛ]
boat (flat-bottomed ~)	**barkë** (f)	[bárkə]
dinghy	**gomone** (f)	[gomónɛ]
lifeboat	**varkë shpëtimi** (f)	[várkə ʃpətími]
motorboat	**skaf** (m)	[skaf]
captain	**kapiten** (m)	[kapitén]
seaman	**marinar** (m)	[marinár]
sailor	**marinar** (m)	[marinár]
crew	**ekip** (m)	[ɛkíp]
boatswain	**kryemarinar** (m)	[kryɛmarinár]
ship's boy	**djali i anijes** (m)	[djáli i aníjɛs]
cook	**kuzhinier** (m)	[kuʒiniér]
ship's doctor	**doktori i anijes** (m)	[doktóri i aníjɛs]
deck	**kuverta** (f)	[kuvérta]
mast	**direk** (m)	[dirék]
sail	**vela** (f)	[véla]
hold	**bagazh** (m)	[bagáʒ]
bow (prow)	**harku sipëror** (m)	[hárku sipərór]

stern	pjesa e pasme (f)	[pjésa ɛ pásmɛ]
oar	rrem (m)	[rɛm]
screw propeller	helikë (f)	[hɛlíkə]

cabin	kabinë (f)	[kabínə]
wardroom	zyrë e oficerëve (m)	[zýrə ɛ ofitsérəvɛ]
engine room	salla e motorit (m)	[sáɫa ɛ motórit]
bridge	urë komanduese (f)	[úrə komandúɛsɛ]
radio room	kabina radiotelegrafike (f)	[kabína radiotɛlɛgrafíkɛ]
wave (radio)	valë (f)	[válə]
logbook	libri i shënimeve (m)	[líbri i ʃənímɛvɛ]

spyglass	dylbi (f)	[dylbí]
bell	këmbanë (f)	[kəmbánə]
flag	flamur (m)	[flamúr]

| hawser (mooring ~) | pallamar (m) | [paɫamár] |
| knot (bowline, etc.) | nyjë (f) | [nýjə] |

| deckrails | parmakë (pl) | [parmákə] |
| gangway | shkallë (f) | [ʃkáɫə] |

anchor	spirancë (f)	[spirántsə]
to weigh anchor	ngre spirancën	[ŋré spirántsən]
to drop anchor	hedh spirancën	[hɛð spirántsən]
anchor chain	zinxhir i spirancës (m)	[zindʒír i spirántsəs]

port (harbor)	port (m)	[port]
quay, wharf	skelë (f)	[skélə]
to berth (moor)	ankoroj	[ankorój]
to cast off	niset	[nísɛt]

trip, voyage	udhëtim (m)	[uðətím]
cruise (sea trip)	udhëtim me krocierë (f)	[uðətím mɛ krotsiérə]
course (route)	kursi i udhëtimit (m)	[kúrsi i uðətímit]
route (itinerary)	itinerar (m)	[itinɛrár]

| fairway (safe water channel) | ujëra të lundrueshme (f) | [újəra tə lundrúɛʃmɛ] |

| shallows | cekëtinë (f) | [tsɛkətínə] |
| to run aground | bllokohet në rërë | [bɫokóhɛt nə rərə] |

storm	stuhi (f)	[stuhí]
signal	sinjal (m)	[siɲál]
to sink (vi)	fundoset	[fundósɛt]
Man overboard!	Njeri në det!	[ɲɛrí nə dɛt!]
SOS (distress signal)	SOS (m)	[sos]
ring buoy	bovë shpëtuese (f)	[bóvə ʃpətúɛsɛ]

CITY

27. Urban transportation

bus	**autobus** (m)	[autobús]
streetcar	**tramvaj** (m)	[tramváj]
trolley bus	**autobus tramvaj** (m)	[autobús tramváj]
route (of bus, etc.)	**itinerar** (m)	[itinɛrárʃ]
number (e.g., bus ~)	**numër** (m)	[númər]
to go by ...	**udhëtoj me ...**	[uðətój mɛ ...]
to get on (~ the bus)	**hip**	[hip]
to get off ...	**zbres ...**	[zbrɛs ...]
stop (e.g., bus ~)	**stacion** (m)	[statsión]
next stop	**stacioni tjetër** (m)	[statsióni tjétər]
terminus	**terminal** (m)	[tɛrminál]
schedule	**orar** (m)	[orárʃ]
to wait (vt)	**pres**	[prɛs]
ticket	**biletë** (f)	[bilétə]
fare	**çmim bilete** (m)	[tʃmím bilétɛ]
cashier (ticket seller)	**shitës biletash** (m)	[ʃítəs bilétaʃ]
ticket inspection	**kontroll biletash** (m)	[kontrółʃ bilétaʃ]
ticket inspector	**kontrollues biletash** (m)	[kontrołúɛs bilétaʃ]
to be late (for ...)	**vonohem**	[vonóhɛm]
to miss (~ the train, etc.)	**humbas**	[humbás]
to be in a hurry	**nxitoj**	[ndzitój]
taxi, cab	**taksi** (m)	[táksi]
taxi driver	**shofer taksie** (m)	[ʃofér taksíɛ]
by taxi	**me taksi**	[mɛ táksi]
taxi stand	**stacion taksish** (m)	[statsión táksiʃ]
to call a taxi	**thërras taksi**	[θərás táksi]
to take a taxi	**marr taksi**	[mar táksi]
traffic	**trafik** (m)	[trafík]
traffic jam	**bllokim trafiku** (m)	[bɬokím trafíku]
rush hour	**orë e trafikut të rëndë** (f)	[órə ɛ trafíkut tə rəndə]
to park (vi)	**parkoj**	[parkój]
to park (vt)	**parkim**	[parkím]
parking lot	**parking** (m)	[parkíɳ]
subway	**metro** (f)	[mɛtró]
station	**stacion** (m)	[statsión]

to take the subway	shkoj me metro	[ʃkoj mɛ métro]
train	tren (m)	[trɛn]
train station	stacion treni (m)	[statsión tréni]

28. City. Life in the city

city, town	qytet (m)	[cytét]
capital city	kryeqytet (m)	[kryɛcytét]
village	fshat (m)	[ffʃát]

city map	hartë e qytetit (f)	[hártə ɛ cytétit]
downtown	qendër e qytetit (f)	[céndər ɛ cytétit]
suburb	periferi (f)	[pɛrifɛrí]
suburban (adj)	periferik	[pɛrifɛrík]

outskirts	periferia (f)	[pɛrifɛría]
environs (suburbs)	periferia (f)	[pɛrifɛría]
city block	bllok pallatesh (m)	[bɫók paɫátɛʃ]
residential block (area)	bllok banimi (m)	[bɫók baními]

traffic	trafik (m)	[trafík]
traffic lights	semafor (m)	[sɛmafór]
public transportation	transport publik (m)	[transpórt publík]
intersection	kryqëzim (m)	[krycəzím]

crosswalk	kalim për këmbësorë (m)	[kalím pər kəmbəsórə]
pedestrian underpass	nënkalim për këmbësorë (m)	[nənkalím pər kəmbəsórə]
to cross (~ the street)	kapërcej	[kapərtséj]
pedestrian	këmbësor (m)	[kəmbəsór]
sidewalk	trotuar (m)	[trotuár]

bridge	urë (f)	[úrə]
embankment (river walk)	breg lumi (m)	[brɛg lúmi]
fountain	shatërvan (m)	[ʃatərván]

allée (garden walkway)	rrugëz (m)	[rúgəz]
park	park (m)	[park]
boulevard	bulevard (m)	[bulɛvárd]
square	shesh (m)	[ʃɛʃ]
avenue (wide street)	bulevard (m)	[bulɛvárd]
street	rrugë (f)	[rúgə]
side street	rrugë dytësore (f)	[rúgə dytəsórɛ]
dead end	rrugë pa krye (f)	[rúgə pa krýɛ]

house	shtëpi (f)	[ʃtəpí]
building	ndërtesë (f)	[ndərtésə]
skyscraper	qiellgërvishtës (m)	[ciɛɫgərvíʃtəs]
facade	fasadë (f)	[fasádə]
roof	çati (f)	[tʃatí]

window	**dritare** (f)	[dritárɛ]
arch	**hark** (m)	[hárk]
column	**kolonë** (f)	[kolónə]
corner	**kënd** (m)	[kǝ́nd]

store window	**vitrinë** (f)	[vitrínə]
signboard (store sign, etc.)	**tabelë** (f)	[tabélə]
poster (e.g., playbill)	**poster** (m)	[postér]
advertising poster	**afishe reklamuese** (f)	[afíʃɛ rɛklamúɛsɛ]
billboard	**tabelë reklamash** (f)	[tabélə rɛklámaʃ]

garbage, trash	**plehra** (f)	[pléhra]
trash can (public ~)	**kosh plehrash** (m)	[koʃ pléhraʃ]
to litter (vi)	**hedh mbeturina**	[hɛð mbɛturína]
garbage dump	**deponi plehrash** (f)	[dɛponí pléhraʃ]

phone booth	**kabinë telefonike** (f)	[kabínə tɛlɛfoníkɛ]
lamppost	**shtyllë dritash** (f)	[ʃtýłə drítaʃ]
bench (park ~)	**stol** (m)	[stol]

police officer	**polic** (m)	[políts]
police	**polici** (f)	[politsí]
beggar	**lypës** (m)	[lýpəs]
homeless (n)	**i pastrehë** (m)	[i pastréhə]

29. Urban institutions

store	**dyqan** (m)	[dycán]
drugstore, pharmacy	**farmaci** (f)	[farmatsí]
eyeglass store	**optikë** (f)	[optíkə]
shopping mall	**qendër tregtare** (f)	[céndər trɛgtárɛ]
supermarket	**supermarket** (m)	[supɛrmarkét]

bakery	**furrë** (f)	[fúrə]
baker	**furrtar** (m)	[furtár]
pastry shop	**pastiçeri** (f)	[pastitʃɛrí]
grocery store	**dyqan ushqimor** (m)	[dycán uʃcimór]
butcher shop	**dyqan mishi** (m)	[dycán míʃi]

| produce store | **dyqan fruta-perimesh** (m) | [dycán frúta-pɛrímɛʃ] |
| market | **treg** (m) | [trɛg] |

coffee house	**kafene** (f)	[kafɛné]
restaurant	**restorant** (m)	[rɛstoránt]
pub, bar	**pab** (m), **pijetore** (f)	[pab], [pijɛtórɛ]
pizzeria	**piceri** (f)	[pitsɛrí]

hair salon	**parukeri** (f)	[parukɛrí]
post office	**zyrë postare** (f)	[zýrə postárɛ]
dry cleaners	**pastrim kimik** (m)	[pastrím kimík]

photo studio	**studio fotografike** (f)	[stúdio fotografíkɛ]
shoe store	**dyqan këpucësh** (m)	[dycán kəpútsəʃ]
bookstore	**librari** (f)	[librarí]
sporting goods store	**dyqan me mallra sportivë** (m)	[dycán mɛ máɫra sportívə]
clothes repair shop	**rrobaqepësi** (f)	[robacɛpəsí]
formal wear rental	**dyqan veshjesh me qira** (m)	[dycán véʃjeʃ mɛ cirá]
video rental store	**dyqan videosh me qira** (m)	[dycán vídɛoʃ mɛ cirá]
circus	**cirk** (m)	[tsírk]
zoo	**kopsht zoologjik** (m)	[kópʃt zoolojík]
movie theater	**kinema** (f)	[kinɛmá]
museum	**muze** (m)	[muzé]
library	**bibliotekë** (f)	[bibliotékə]
theater	**teatër** (m)	[tɛátər]
opera (opera house)	**opera** (f)	[opéra]
nightclub	**klub nate** (m)	[klúb nátɛ]
casino	**kazino** (f)	[kazíno]
mosque	**xhami** (f)	[dʒamí]
synagogue	**sinagogë** (f)	[sinagógə]
cathedral	**katedrale** (f)	[katɛdrálɛ]
temple	**tempull** (m)	[témpuɫ]
church	**kishë** (f)	[kíʃə]
college	**kolegj** (m)	[koléj]
university	**universitet** (m)	[univɛrsitét]
school	**shkollë** (f)	[ʃkóɫə]
prefecture	**prefekturë** (f)	[prɛfɛktúrə]
city hall	**bashki** (f)	[baʃkí]
hotel	**hotel** (m)	[hotél]
bank	**bankë** (f)	[bánkə]
embassy	**ambasadë** (f)	[ambasádə]
travel agency	**agjenci udhëtimesh** (f)	[ajɛntsí uðətímɛʃ]
information office	**zyrë informacioni** (f)	[zýrə informatsióni]
currency exchange	**këmbim valutor** (m)	[kəmbím valutór]
subway	**metro** (f)	[mɛtró]
hospital	**spital** (m)	[spitál]
gas station	**pikë karburanti** (f)	[píkə karburánti]
parking lot	**parking** (m)	[parkíŋ]

30. Signs

signboard (store sign, etc.)	**tabelë** (f)	[tabélə]
notice (door sign, etc.)	**njoftim** (m)	[ɲoftím]
poster	**poster** (m)	[postér]
direction sign	**tabelë drejtuese** (f)	[tabélə drɛjtúɛsɛ]
arrow (sign)	**shigjetë** (f)	[ʃiɟétə]
caution	**kujdes** (m)	[kujdés]
warning sign	**shenjë paralajmëruese** (f)	[ʃéɲə paralajmərúɛsɛ]
to warn (vt)	**paralajmëroj**	[paralajmərój]
rest day (weekly ~)	**ditë pushimi** (f)	[dítə puʃími]
timetable (schedule)	**orar** (m)	[orár]
opening hours	**orari i punës** (m)	[orári i púnəs]
WELCOME!	**MIRË SE VINI!**	[mírə sɛ víni!]
ENTRANCE	**HYRJE**	[hýrjɛ]
EXIT	**DALJE**	[dáljɛ]
PUSH	**SHTY**	[ʃty]
PULL	**TËRHIQ**	[tərhíc]
OPEN	**HAPUR**	[hápur]
CLOSED	**MBYLLUR**	[mbýɫur]
WOMEN	**GRA**	[gra]
MEN	**BURRA**	[búra]
DISCOUNTS	**ZBRITJE**	[zbrítjɛ]
SALE	**ULJE**	[úljɛ]
NEW!	**TË REJA!**	[tə réja!]
FREE	**FALAS**	[fálas]
ATTENTION!	**KUJDES!**	[kujdés!]
NO VACANCIES	**NUK KA VENDE TË LIRA**	[nuk ka véndɛ tə líra]
RESERVED	**E REZERVUAR**	[ɛ rɛzɛrvúar]
ADMINISTRATION	**ADMINISTRATA**	[administráta]
STAFF ONLY	**VETËM PËR STAFIN**	[vétəm pər stáfin]
BEWARE OF THE DOG!	**RUHUNI NGA QENI!**	[rúhuni ŋa céni!]
NO SMOKING	**NDALOHET DUHANI**	[ndalóhɛt duháni]
DO NOT TOUCH!	**MOS PREK!**	[mos prék!]
DANGEROUS	**TË RREZIKSHME**	[tə rɛzíkʃmɛ]
DANGER	**RREZIK**	[rɛzík]
HIGH VOLTAGE	**TENSION I LARTË**	[tɛnsión i lártə]
NO SWIMMING!	**NUK LEJOHET NOTI!**	[nuk lɛjóhɛt nóti!]
OUT OF ORDER	**E PRISHUR**	[ɛ príʃur]
FLAMMABLE	**LËNDË DJEGËSE**	[ləndə djégəsɛ]
FORBIDDEN	**E NDALUAR**	[ɛ ndalúar]

| NO TRESPASSING! | **NDALOHET HYRJA** | [ndalóhɛt hýrja] |
| WET PAINT | **BOJË E FRESKËT** | [bójə ɛ fréskət] |

31. Shopping

to buy (purchase)	**blej**	[blɛj]
purchase	**blerje** (f)	[blérjɛ]
to go shopping	**shkoj për pazar**	[ʃkoj pər pazár]
shopping	**pazar** (m)	[pazár]

| to be open (ab. store) | **hapur** | [hápur] |
| to be closed | **mbyllur** | [mbýɫur] |

footwear, shoes	**këpucë** (f)	[kəpútsə]
clothes, clothing	**veshje** (f)	[véʃjɛ]
cosmetics	**kozmetikë** (f)	[kozmɛtíkə]
food products	**mallra ushqimore** (f)	[máɫra uʃcimórɛ]
gift, present	**dhuratë** (f)	[ðurátə]

| salesman | **shitës** (m) | [ʃítəs] |
| saleswoman | **shitëse** (f) | [ʃítəsɛ] |

check out, cash desk	**arkë** (f)	[árkə]
mirror	**pasqyrë** (f)	[pascýrə]
counter (store ~)	**banak** (m)	[bának]
fitting room	**dhomë prove** (f)	[ðómə próvɛ]

to try on	**provoj**	[provój]
to fit (ab. dress, etc.)	**më rri mirë**	[mə ri mírə]
to like (I like ...)	**pëlqej**	[pəlcéj]

price	**çmim** (m)	[tʃmím]
price tag	**etiketa e çmimit** (f)	[ɛtikéta ɛ tʃmímit]
to cost (vt)	**kushton**	[kuʃtón]
How much?	**Sa?**	[sa?]
discount	**ulje** (f)	[úljɛ]

inexpensive (adj)	**jo e shtrenjtë**	[jo ɛ ʃtréɲtə]
cheap (adj)	**e lirë**	[ɛ lírə]
expensive (adj)	**i shtrenjtë**	[i ʃtréɲtə]
It's expensive	**Është e shtrenjtë**	[əʃtə ɛ ʃtréɲtə]

rental (n)	**qiramarrje** (f)	[ciramárjɛ]
to rent (~ a tuxedo)	**marr me qira**	[mar mɛ cirá]
credit (trade credit)	**kredit** (m)	[krɛdít]
on credit (adv)	**me kredi**	[mɛ krɛdí]

CLOTHING & ACCESSORIES

32. Outerwear. Coats

clothes	**rroba** (f)	[róba]
outerwear	**veshje e sipërme** (f)	[véʃjɛ ɛ sípərmɛ]
winter clothing	**veshje dimri** (f)	[véʃjɛ dímri]
coat (overcoat)	**pallto** (f)	[páɫto]
fur coat	**gëzof** (m)	[gəzóf]
fur jacket	**xhaketë lëkure** (f)	[dʒakétə ləkúrɛ]
down coat	**xhup** (m)	[dʒup]
jacket (e.g., leather ~)	**xhaketë** (f)	[dʒakétə]
raincoat (trenchcoat, etc.)	**pardesy** (f)	[pardɛsý]
waterproof (adj)	**kundër shiut**	[kúndər ʃíut]

33. Men's & women's clothing

shirt (button shirt)	**këmishë** (f)	[kəmíʃə]
pants	**pantallona** (f)	[pantaɫóna]
jeans	**xhinse** (f)	[dʒínsɛ]
suit jacket	**xhaketë kostumi** (f)	[dʒakétə kostúmi]
suit	**kostum** (m)	[kostúm]
dress (frock)	**fustan** (m)	[fustán]
skirt	**fund** (m)	[fund]
blouse	**bluzë** (f)	[blúzə]
knitted jacket (cardigan, etc.)	**xhaketë me thurje** (f)	[dʒakétə mɛ θúrjɛ]
jacket (of woman's suit)	**xhaketë femrash** (f)	[dʒakétə fémraʃ]
T-shirt	**bluzë** (f)	[blúzə]
shorts (short trousers)	**pantallona të shkurtra** (f)	[pantaɫóna tə ʃkúrtra]
tracksuit	**tuta sportive** (f)	[túta sportívɛ]
bathrobe	**peshqir trupi** (m)	[pɛʃɕír trúpi]
pajamas	**pizhame** (f)	[piʒámɛ]
sweater	**triko** (f)	[tríko]
pullover	**pulovër** (m)	[pulóvər]
vest	**jelek** (m)	[jɛlék]
tailcoat	**frak** (m)	[frak]
tuxedo	**smoking** (m)	[smokíŋ]

uniform	**uniformë** (f)	[unifórmə]
workwear	**rroba pune** (f)	[róba púnɛ]
overalls	**kominoshe** (f)	[kominóʃɛ]
coat (e.g., doctor's smock)	**uniformë** (f)	[unifórmə]

34. Clothing. Underwear

underwear	**të brendshme** (f)	[tə bréndʃmɛ]
boxers, briefs	**boksera** (f)	[bokséra]
panties	**brekë** (f)	[brékə]
undershirt (A-shirt)	**fanellë** (f)	[fanéłə]
socks	**çorape** (pl)	[tʃorápɛ]
nightdress	**këmishë nate** (f)	[kəmíʃə nátɛ]
bra	**sytjena** (f)	[sytjéna]
knee highs (knee-high socks)	**çorape déri tek gjuri** (pl)	[tʃorápɛ déri ték ɟúri]
pantyhose	**geta** (f)	[géta]
stockings (thigh highs)	**çorape të holla** (pl)	[tʃorápɛ tə hóła]
bathing suit	**rrobë banje** (f)	[róbə báɲɛ]

35. Headwear

hat	**kapelë** (f)	[kapélə]
fedora	**kapelë republike** (f)	[kapélə rɛpublíkɛ]
baseball cap	**kapelë bejsbolli** (f)	[kapélə bɛjsbółi]
flatcap	**kapelë e sheshtë** (f)	[kapélə ɛ ʃéʃtə]
beret	**beretë** (f)	[bɛrétə]
hood	**kapuç** (m)	[kapútʃ]
panama hat	**kapelë panama** (f)	[kapélə panamá]
knit cap (knitted hat)	**kapuç leshi** (m)	[kapútʃ léʃi]
headscarf	**shami** (f)	[ʃamí]
women's hat	**kapelë femrash** (f)	[kapélə fémraʃ]
hard hat	**helmetë** (f)	[hɛlmétə]
garrison cap	**kapelë ushtrie** (f)	[kapélə uʃtríɛ]
helmet	**helmetë** (f)	[hɛlmétə]
derby	**kapelë derby** (f)	[kapélə dérby]
top hat	**kapelë cilindër** (f)	[kapélə tsilíndər]

36. Footwear

footwear	**këpucë** (pl)	[kəpútsə]
shoes (men's shoes)	**këpucë burrash** (pl)	[kəpútsə búraʃ]

shoes (women's shoes)	këpucë grash (pl)	[kəpútsə gráʃ]
boots (e.g., cowboy ~)	çizme (pl)	[tʃízmɛ]
slippers	pantofla (pl)	[pantófla]

| tennis shoes (e.g., Nike ~) | atlete tenisi (pl) | [atlétɛ tɛnísi] |
| sneakers (e.g., Converse ~) | atlete (pl) | [atlétɛ] |

| sandals | sandale (pl) | [sandálɛ] |

cobbler (shoe repairer)	këpucëtar (m)	[kəputsətár]
heel	takë (f)	[tákə]
pair (of shoes)	palë (f)	[pálə]

shoestring	lidhëse këpucësh (f)	[líðəsɛ kəpútsəʃ]
to lace (vt)	lidh këpucët	[lið kəpútsət]
shoehorn	lugë këpucësh (f)	[lúgə kəpútsəʃ]
shoe polish	bojë këpucësh (f)	[bójə kəpútsəʃ]

37. Personal accessories

gloves	dorëza (pl)	[dórəza]
mittens	doreza (f)	[doréza]
scarf (muffler)	shall (m)	[ʃaɫ]

glasses (eyeglasses)	syze (f)	[sýzɛ]
frame (eyeglass ~)	skelet syzesh (m)	[skɛlét sýzɛʃ]
umbrella	çadër (f)	[tʃádər]
walking stick	bastun (m)	[bastún]

| hairbrush | furçë flokësh (f) | [fúrtʃə flókəʃ] |
| fan | erashkë (f) | [ɛráʃkə] |

| tie (necktie) | kravatë (f) | [kravátə] |
| bow tie | papion (m) | [papión] |

| suspenders | aski (pl) | [askí] |
| handkerchief | shami (f) | [ʃamí] |

| comb | krehër (m) | [kréhər] |
| barrette | kapëse flokësh (f) | [kápəsɛ flókəʃ] |

| hairpin | karficë (f) | [karfítsə] |
| buckle | tokëz (f) | [tókəz] |

| belt | rrip (m) | [rip] |
| shoulder strap | rrip supi (m) | [rip súpi] |

bag (handbag)	çantë dore (f)	[tʃántə dórɛ]
purse	çantë (f)	[tʃántə]
backpack	çantë shpine (f)	[tʃántə ʃpínɛ]

38. Clothing. Miscellaneous

fashion	**modë** (f)	[módǝ]
in vogue (adj)	**në modë**	[nǝ módǝ]
fashion designer	**stilist** (m)	[stilíst]
collar	**jakë** (f)	[jákǝ]
pocket	**xhep** (m)	[dʒɛp]
pocket (as adj)	**i xhepit**	[i dʒépit]
sleeve	**mëngë** (f)	[méŋǝ]
hanging loop	**hallkë për varje** (f)	[háɫkǝ pǝr várjɛ]
fly (on trousers)	**zinxhir** (m)	[zindʒír]
zipper (fastener)	**zinxhir** (m)	[zindʒír]
fastener	**kapëse** (f)	[kápǝsɛ]
button	**kopsë** (f)	[kópsǝ]
buttonhole	**vrimë kopse** (f)	[vrímǝ kópsɛ]
to come off (ab. button)	**këputet**	[kǝpútɛt]
to sew (vi, vt)	**qep**	[cɛp]
to embroider (vi, vt)	**qëndis**	[cǝndís]
embroidery	**qëndisje** (f)	[cǝndísjɛ]
sewing needle	**gjilpërë për qepje** (f)	[ɟilpérǝ pǝr cépjɛ]
thread	**pe** (m)	[pɛ]
seam	**tegel** (m)	[tɛgél]
to get dirty (vi)	**bëhem pis**	[bǝhɛm pis]
stain (mark, spot)	**njollë** (f)	[ɲóɫǝ]
to crease, crumple (vi)	**zhubros**	[ʒubrós]
to tear, to rip (vt)	**gris**	[gris]
clothes moth	**molë rrobash** (f)	[mólǝ róbaʃ]

39. Personal care. Cosmetics

toothpaste	**pastë dhëmbësh** (f)	[pástǝ ðémbǝʃ]
toothbrush	**furçë dhëmbësh** (f)	[fúrtʃǝ ðémbǝʃ]
to brush one's teeth	**laj dhëmbët**	[laj ðémbǝt]
razor	**brisk** (m)	[brísk]
shaving cream	**pastë rroje** (f)	[pástǝ rójɛ]
to shave (vi)	**rruhem**	[rúhɛm]
soap	**sapun** (m)	[sapún]
shampoo	**shampo** (f)	[ʃampó]
scissors	**gërshërë** (f)	[gǝrʃérǝ]
nail file	**limë thonjsh** (f)	[límǝ θóɲʃ]
nail clippers	**prerëse thonjsh** (f)	[prérǝsɛ θóɲʃ]
tweezers	**piskatore vetullash** (f)	[piskatórɛ vétuɫaʃ]

cosmetics	**kozmetikë** (f)	[kozmεtíkə]
face mask	**maskë fytyre** (f)	[máskə fytýrε]
manicure	**manikyr** (m)	[manikýr]
to have a manicure	**bëj manikyr**	[bəj manikýr]
pedicure	**pedikyr** (m)	[pεdikýr]

make-up bag	**çantë kozmetike** (f)	[tʃántə kozmεtíkε]
face powder	**pudër fytyre** (f)	[púdər fytýrε]
powder compact	**pudër kompakte** (f)	[púdər kompáktε]
blusher	**ruzh** (m)	[ruʒ]

perfume (bottled)	**parfum** (m)	[parfúm]
toilet water (lotion)	**parfum** (m)	[parfúm]
lotion	**krem** (m)	[krεm]
cologne	**kolonjë** (f)	[kolóɲə]

eyeshadow	**rimel** (m)	[rimél]
eyeliner	**laps për sy** (m)	[láps pər sy]
mascara	**rimel** (m)	[rimél]

lipstick	**buzëkuq** (m)	[buzəkúc]
nail polish, enamel	**llak për thonj** (m)	[ɬak pər θóɲ]
hair spray	**llak flokësh** (m)	[ɬak flókəʃ]
deodorant	**deodorant** (m)	[dεodoránt]

cream	**krem** (m)	[krεm]
face cream	**krem për fytyrë** (m)	[krεm pər fytýrə]
hand cream	**krem për duar** (m)	[krεm pər dúar]
anti-wrinkle cream	**krem kundër rrudhave** (m)	[krεm kúndər rúðavε]
day cream	**krem dite** (m)	[krεm dítε]
night cream	**krem nate** (m)	[krεm nátε]
day (as adj)	**dite**	[dítε]
night (as adj)	**nate**	[nátε]

tampon	**tampon** (m)	[tampón]
toilet paper (toilet roll)	**letër higjienike** (f)	[létər hiɟiεníkε]
hair dryer	**tharëse flokësh** (f)	[θárəsε flókəʃ]

40. Watches. Clocks

watch (wristwatch)	**orë dore** (f)	[órə dórε]
dial	**faqe e orës** (f)	[fácε ε órəs]
hand (of clock, watch)	**akrep** (m)	[akrép]
metal watch band	**rrip metalik ore** (m)	[rip mεtalík órε]
watch strap	**rrip ore** (m)	[rip órε]

battery	**bateri** (f)	[batεrí]
to be dead (battery)	**e shkarkuar**	[ε ʃkarkúar]
to change a battery	**ndërroj baterinë**	[ndərój batεrínə]
to run fast	**kalon shpejt**	[kalón ʃpéjt]

to run slow	ngel prapa	[ŋɛl prápa]
wall clock	orë muri (f)	[órə múri]
hourglass	orë rëre (f)	[órə rərɛ]
sundial	orë diellore (f)	[órə diɛɫórɛ]
alarm clock	orë me zile (f)	[órə mɛ zílɛ]
watchmaker	orëndreqës (m)	[orəndrécəs]
to repair (vt)	ndreq	[ndréc]

EVERYDAY EXPERIENCE

41. Money

money	**para** (f)	[pará]
currency exchange	**këmbim valutor** (m)	[kəmbím valutór]
exchange rate	**kurs këmbimi** (m)	[kurs kəmbími]
ATM	**bankomat** (m)	[bankomát]
coin	**monedhë** (f)	[monéðə]
dollar	**dollar** (m)	[doɫár]
euro	**euro** (f)	[éuro]
lira	**lirë** (f)	[lírə]
Deutschmark	**Marka gjermane** (f)	[márka ɟɛrmánɛ]
franc	**franga** (f)	[fráŋa]
pound sterling	**sterlina angleze** (f)	[stɛrlína aŋlézɛ]
yen	**jen** (m)	[jén]
debt	**borxh** (m)	[bórdʒ]
debtor	**debitor** (m)	[dɛbitór]
to lend (money)	**jap hua**	[jap huá]
to borrow (vi, vt)	**marr hua**	[mar huá]
bank	**bankë** (f)	[bánkə]
account	**llogari** (f)	[ɫogarí]
to deposit (vt)	**depozitoj**	[dɛpozitój]
to deposit into the account	**depozitoj në llogari**	[dɛpozitój nə ɫogarí]
to withdraw (vt)	**tërheq**	[tərhéc]
credit card	**kartë krediti** (f)	[kártə krɛdíti]
cash	**kesh** (m)	[kɛʃ]
check	**çek** (m)	[tʃɛk]
to write a check	**lëshoj një çek**	[ləʃój ɲə tʃék]
checkbook	**bllok çeqesh** (m)	[bɫók tʃécɛʃ]
wallet	**portofol** (m)	[portofól]
change purse	**kuletë** (f)	[kulétə]
safe	**kasafortë** (f)	[kasafórtə]
heir	**trashëgimtar** (m)	[traʃəgimtár]
inheritance	**trashëgimi** (f)	[traʃəgimí]
fortune (wealth)	**pasuri** (f)	[pasurí]
lease	**qira** (f)	[cirá]
rent (money)	**qiraja** (f)	[cirája]

to rent (sth from sb)	**marr me qira**	[mar mɛ cirá]
price	**çmim** (m)	[tʃmím]
cost	**kosto** (f)	[kósto]
sum	**shumë** (f)	[ʃúmə]
to spend (vt)	**shpenzoj**	[ʃpɛnzój]
expenses	**shpenzime** (f)	[ʃpɛnzímɛ]
to economize (vi, vt)	**kursej**	[kurséj]
economical	**ekonomik**	[ɛkonomík]
to pay (vi, vt)	**paguaj**	[pagúaj]
payment	**pagesë** (f)	[pagésə]
change (give the ~)	**kusur** (m)	[kusúr]
tax	**taksë** (f)	[táksə]
fine	**gjobë** (f)	[ɟóbə]
to fine (vt)	**vendos gjobë**	[vɛndós ɟóbə]

42. Post. Postal service

post office	**zyrë postare** (f)	[zýrə postárɛ]
mail (letters, etc.)	**postë** (f)	[póstə]
mailman	**postier** (m)	[postiér]
opening hours	**orari i punës** (m)	[orári i púnəs]
letter	**letër** (f)	[létər]
registered letter	**letër rekomande** (f)	[létər rɛkomándɛ]
postcard	**kartolinë** (f)	[kartolínə]
telegram	**telegram** (m)	[tɛlɛgrám]
package (parcel)	**pako** (f)	[páko]
money transfer	**transfer parash** (m)	[transfér paráʃ]
to receive (vt)	**pranoj**	[pranój]
to send (vt)	**dërgoj**	[dərgój]
sending	**dërgesë** (f)	[dərgésə]
address	**adresë** (f)	[adrésə]
ZIP code	**kodi postar** (m)	[kódi postár]
sender	**dërguesi** (m)	[dərgúɛsi]
receiver	**pranues** (m)	[pranúɛs]
name (first name)	**emër** (m)	[émər]
surname (last name)	**mbiemër** (m)	[mbiémər]
postage rate	**tarifë postare** (f)	[tarífə postárɛ]
standard (adj)	**standard**	[standárd]
economical (adj)	**ekonomike**	[ɛkonomíkɛ]
weight	**peshë** (f)	[péʃə]
to weigh (~ letters)	**peshoj**	[pɛʃój]

envelope	**zarf** (m)	[zarf]
postage stamp	**pullë postare** (f)	[púłə postárɛ]
to stamp an envelope	**vendos pullën postare**	[vɛndós púłən postárɛ]

43. Banking

bank	**bankë** (f)	[bánkə]
branch (of bank, etc.)	**degë** (f)	[dégə]
bank clerk, consultant	**punonjës banke** (m)	[punóɲəs bánkɛ]
manager (director)	**drejtor** (m)	[drɛjtór]
bank account	**llogari bankare** (f)	[łogarí bankárɛ]
account number	**numër llogarie** (m)	[númər łogaríɛ]
checking account	**llogari rrjedhëse** (f)	[łogarí rjéðəsɛ]
savings account	**llogari kursimesh** (f)	[łogarí kursímɛʃ]
to open an account	**hap një llogari**	[hap ɲə łogarí]
to close the account	**mbyll një llogari**	[mbýł ɲə łogarí]
to deposit into the account	**depozitoj në llogari**	[dɛpozitój nə łogarí]
to withdraw (vt)	**tërheq**	[tərhéc]
deposit	**depozitë** (f)	[dɛpozítə]
to make a deposit	**kryej një depozitim**	[krýɛj ɲə dɛpozitím]
wire transfer	**transfer bankar** (m)	[transfér bankár]
to wire, to transfer	**transferoj para**	[transfɛrój pará]
sum	**shumë** (f)	[ʃúmə]
How much?	**Sa?**	[sa?]
signature	**nënshkrim** (m)	[nənʃkrím]
to sign (vt)	**nënshkruaj**	[nənʃkrúaj]
credit card	**kartë krediti** (f)	[kártə krɛdíti]
code (PIN code)	**kodi PIN** (m)	[kódi pin]
credit card number	**numri i kartës**	[númri i kártəs
	së kreditit (m)	sə krɛdítit]
ATM	**bankomat** (m)	[bankomát]
check	**çek** (m)	[tʃɛk]
to write a check	**lëshoj një çek**	[ləʃój ɲə tʃék]
checkbook	**bllok çeqesh** (m)	[błók tʃécɛʃ]
loan (bank ~)	**kredi** (f)	[krɛdí]
to apply for a loan	**aplikoj për kredi**	[aplikój pər krɛdí]
to get a loan	**marr kredi**	[mar krɛdí]
to give a loan	**jap kredi**	[jap krɛdí]
guarantee	**garanci** (f)	[garantsí]

44. Telephone. Phone conversation

telephone	**telefon** (m)	[tɛlɛfón]
cell phone	**celular** (m)	[tsɛlulár]
answering machine	**sekretari telefonike** (f)	[sɛkrɛtarí tɛlɛfoníkɛ]
to call (by phone)	**telefonoj**	[tɛlɛfonój]
phone call	**telefonatë** (f)	[tɛlɛfonátə]
to dial a number	**i bie numrit**	[i bíɛ númrit]
Hello!	**Përshëndetje!**	[pərʃəndétjɛ!]
to ask (vt)	**pyes**	[pýɛs]
to answer (vi, vt)	**përgjigjem**	[pərɟíɟɛm]
to hear (vt)	**dëgjoj**	[dəɟój]
well (adv)	**mirë**	[mírə]
not well (adv)	**jo mirë**	[jo mírə]
noises (interference)	**zhurmë** (f)	[ʒúrmə]
receiver	**marrës** (m)	[márəs]
to pick up (~ the phone)	**ngre telefonin**	[ŋré tɛlɛfónin]
to hang up (~ the phone)	**mbyll telefonin**	[mbýɫ tɛlɛfónin]
busy (engaged)	**i zënë**	[i zénə]
to ring (ab. phone)	**bie zilja**	[bíɛ zílja]
telephone book	**numerator telefonik** (m)	[numɛratór tɛlɛfoník]
local (adj)	**lokale**	[lokálɛ]
local call	**thirrje lokale** (f)	[θírjɛ lokálɛ]
long distance (~ call)	**distancë e largët**	[distántsə ɛ lárgət]
long-distance call	**thirrje në distancë** (f)	[θírjɛ nə distántsə]
international (adj)	**ndërkombëtar**	[ndərkombətár]
international call	**thirrje ndërkombëtare** (f)	[θírjɛ ndərkombətárɛ]

45. Cell phone

cell phone	**celular** (m)	[tsɛlulár]
display	**ekran** (m)	[ɛkrán]
button	**buton** (m)	[butón]
SIM card	**karta SIM** (m)	[kárta sim]
battery	**bateri** (f)	[batɛrí]
to be dead (battery)	**e shkarkuar**	[ɛ ʃkarkúar]
charger	**karikues** (m)	[karikúɛs]
menu	**menu** (f)	[mɛnú]
settings	**parametra** (f)	[paramétra]
tune (melody)	**melodi** (f)	[mɛlodí]
to select (vt)	**përzgjedh**	[pərzɟéð]

calculator	makinë llogaritëse (f)	[makínə ɫogarítəsɛ]
voice mail	postë zanore (f)	[póstə zanórɛ]
alarm clock	alarm (m)	[alárm]
contacts	kontakte (pl)	[kontáktɛ]

| SMS (text message) | SMS (m) | [ɛsɛmɛs] |
| subscriber | abonent (m) | [abonént] |

46. Stationery

| ballpoint pen | stilolaps (m) | [stiloláps] |
| fountain pen | stilograf (m) | [stilográf] |

pencil	laps (m)	[láps]
highlighter	shënjues (m)	[ʃəɲúɛs]
felt-tip pen	tushë me bojë (f)	[túʃə mɛ bójə]

| notepad | bllok shënimesh (m) | [bɫók ʃənímɛʃ] |
| agenda (diary) | agjendë (f) | [aɟéndə] |

ruler	vizore (f)	[vizórɛ]
calculator	makinë llogaritëse (f)	[makínə ɫogarítəsɛ]
eraser	gomë (f)	[gómə]
thumbtack	pineskë (f)	[pinéskə]
paper clip	kapëse fletësh (f)	[kápəsɛ flétəʃ]

glue	ngjitës (m)	[nɟítəs]
stapler	ngjitës metalik (m)	[nɟítəs mɛtalík]
hole punch	hapës vrimash (m)	[hápəs vrímaʃ]
pencil sharpener	mprehëse lapsash (m)	[mpréhəsɛ lápsaʃ]

47. Foreign languages

language	gjuhë (f)	[ɟúhə]
foreign (adj)	huaj	[húaj]
foreign language	gjuhë e huaj (f)	[ɟúhə ɛ húaj]
to study (vt)	studioj	[studiój]
to learn (language, etc.)	mësoj	[məsój]

to read (vi, vt)	lexoj	[lɛdzój]
to speak (vi, vt)	flas	[flas]
to understand (vt)	kuptoj	[kuptój]
to write (vt)	shkruaj	[ʃkrúaj]

fast (adv)	shpejt	[ʃpɛjt]
slowly (adv)	ngadalë	[ŋadálə]
fluently (adv)	rrjedhshëm	[rjéðʃəm]
rules	rregullat (pl)	[réguɫat]

grammar	gramatikë (f)	[gramatíkə]
vocabulary	fjalor (m)	[fjalór]
phonetics	fonetikë (f)	[fonɛtíkə]

textbook	tekst mësimor (m)	[tɛkst məsimór]
dictionary	fjalor (m)	[fjalór]
teach-yourself book	libër i mësimit autodidakt (m)	[líbər i məsímit autodidákt]
phrasebook	libër frazeologjik (m)	[líbər frazɛoloɟík]

cassette, tape	kasetë (f)	[kasétə]
videotape	videokasetë (f)	[vidɛokasétə]
CD, compact disc	CD (f)	[tsɛdé]
DVD	DVD (m)	[dividí]

alphabet	alfabet (m)	[alfabét]
to spell (vt)	gërmëzoj	[gərməzój]
pronunciation	shqiptim (m)	[ʃciptím]

accent	aksent (m)	[aksént]
with an accent	me aksent	[mɛ aksént]
without an accent	pa aksent	[pa aksént]

| word | fjalë (f) | [fjálə] |
| meaning | kuptim (m) | [kuptím] |

course (e.g., a French ~)	kurs (m)	[kurs]
to sign up	regjistrohem	[rɛɟistróhɛm]
teacher	mësues (m)	[məsúɛs]

translation (process)	përkthim (m)	[pərkθím]
translation (text, etc.)	përkthim (m)	[pərkθím]
translator	përkthyes (m)	[pərkθýɛs]
interpreter	përkthyes (m)	[pərkθýɛs]

| polyglot | poliglot (m) | [poliglót] |
| memory | kujtesë (f) | [kujtésə] |

MEALS. RESTAURANT

48. Table setting

spoon	**lugë** (f)	[lúgə]
knife	**thikë** (f)	[θíkə]
fork	**pirun** (m)	[pirún]
cup (e.g., coffee ~)	**filxhan** (m)	[fildʒán]
plate (dinner ~)	**pjatë** (f)	[pjátə]
saucer	**pjatë filxhani** (f)	[pjátə fildʒáni]
napkin (on table)	**pecetë** (f)	[pɛtsétə]
toothpick	**kruajtëse dhëmbësh** (f)	[krúajtəsɛ ðémbəʃ]

49. Restaurant

restaurant	**restorant** (m)	[rɛstoránt]
coffee house	**kafene** (f)	[kafɛné]
pub, bar	**pab** (m), **pijetore** (f)	[pab], [pijɛtórɛ]
tearoom	**çajtore** (f)	[tʃajtórɛ]
waiter	**kamerier** (m)	[kamɛriér]
waitress	**kameriere** (f)	[kamɛriérɛ]
bartender	**banakier** (m)	[banakiér]
menu	**menu** (f)	[mɛnú]
wine list	**menu verërash** (f)	[mɛnú vérəraʃ]
to book a table	**rezervoj një tavolinë**	[rɛzɛrvój ɲə tavolínə]
course, dish	**pjatë** (f)	[pjátə]
to order (meal)	**porosis**	[porosís]
to make an order	**bëj porosinë**	[bəj porosínə]
aperitif	**aperitiv** (m)	[apɛritív]
appetizer	**antipastë** (f)	[antipástə]
dessert	**ëmbëlsirë** (f)	[əmbəlsírə]
check	**faturë** (f)	[fatúrə]
to pay the check	**paguaj faturën**	[pagúaj fatúrən]
to give change	**jap kusur**	[jap kusúr]
tip	**bakshish** (m)	[bakʃíʃ]

50. Meals

food	**ushqim** (m)	[uʃcím]
to eat (vi, vt)	**ha**	[ha]
breakfast	**mëngjes** (m)	[mənɟés]
to have breakfast	**ha mëngjes**	[ha mənɟés]
lunch	**drekë** (f)	[drékə]
to have lunch	**ha drekë**	[ha drékə]
dinner	**darkë** (f)	[dárkə]
to have dinner	**ha darkë**	[ha dárkə]
appetite	**oreks** (m)	[oréks]
Enjoy your meal!	**Të bëftë mirë!**	[tə bəftə mírə!]
to open (~ a bottle)	**hap**	[hap]
to spill (liquid)	**derdh**	[dérð]
to spill out (vi)	**derdhje**	[dérðjɛ]
to boil (vi)	**ziej**	[zíɛj]
to boil (vt)	**ziej**	[zíɛj]
boiled (~ water)	**i zier**	[i zíɛr]
to chill, cool down (vt)	**ftoh**	[ftoh]
to chill (vi)	**ftohje**	[ftóhjɛ]
taste, flavor	**shije** (f)	[ʃíjɛ]
aftertaste	**shije** (f)	[ʃíjɛ]
to slim down (lose weight)	**dobësohem**	[dobəsóhɛm]
diet	**dietë** (f)	[diétə]
vitamin	**vitaminë** (f)	[vitamínə]
calorie	**kalori** (f)	[kalorí]
vegetarian (n)	**vegjetarian** (m)	[vɛɟɛtarián]
vegetarian (adj)	**vegjetarian**	[vɛɟɛtarián]
fats (nutrient)	**yndyrë** (f)	[yndýrə]
proteins	**proteinë** (f)	[protɛínə]
carbohydrates	**karbohidrat** (m)	[karbohidrát]
slice (of lemon, ham)	**fetë** (f)	[fétə]
piece (of cake, pie)	**copë** (f)	[tsópə]
crumb (of bread, cake, etc.)	**dromcë** (f)	[drómtsə]

51. Cooked dishes

course, dish	**pjatë** (f)	[pjátə]
cuisine	**kuzhinë** (f)	[kuʒínə]
recipe	**recetë** (f)	[rɛtsétə]

portion	racion (m)	[ratsión]
salad	sallatë (f)	[saɫátə]
soup	supë (f)	[súpə]
clear soup (broth)	lëng mishi (m)	[ləŋ míʃi]
sandwich (bread)	sandviç (m)	[sandvítʃ]
fried eggs	vezë të skuqura (pl)	[vézə tə skúcura]
hamburger (beefburger)	hamburger	[hamburgér]
beefsteak	biftek (m)	[bifték]
side dish	garniturë (f)	[garnitúrə]
spaghetti	shpageti (pl)	[ʃpagéti]
mashed potatoes	pure patatesh (f)	[puré patátɛʃ]
pizza	pica (f)	[pítsa]
porridge (oatmeal, etc.)	qull (m)	[cuɫ]
omelet	omëletë (f)	[oməlétə]
boiled (e.g., ~ beef)	i zier	[i zíɛr]
smoked (adj)	i tymosur	[i tymósur]
fried (adj)	i skuqur	[i skúcur]
dried (adj)	i tharë	[i θárə]
frozen (adj)	i ngrirë	[i ŋrírə]
pickled (adj)	i marinuar	[i marinúar]
sweet (sugary)	i ëmbël	[i ə́mbəl]
salty (adj)	i kripur	[i krípur]
cold (adj)	i ftohtë	[i ftóhtə]
hot (adj)	i nxehtë	[i ndzéhtə]
bitter (adj)	i hidhur	[i híður]
tasty (adj)	i shijshëm	[i ʃíʃəm]
to cook in boiling water	ziej	[zíɛj]
to cook (dinner)	gatuaj	[gatúaj]
to fry (vt)	skuq	[skuc]
to heat up (food)	ngroh	[ŋróh]
to salt (vt)	hedh kripë	[hɛð krípə]
to pepper (vt)	hedh piper	[hɛð pipér]
to grate (vt)	rendoj	[rɛndój]
peel (n)	lëkurë (f)	[ləkúrə]
to peel (vt)	qëroj	[cərój]

52. Food

meat	mish (m)	[miʃ]
chicken	pulë (f)	[púlə]
Rock Cornish hen (poussin)	mish pule (m)	[miʃ púlɛ]
duck	rosë (f)	[rósə]

goose	patë (f)	[pátə]
game	gjah (m)	[ɟáh]
turkey	mish gjel deti (m)	[miʃ ɟɛl déti]

pork	mish derri (m)	[miʃ déri]
veal	mish viçi (m)	[miʃ vítʃi]
lamb	mish qengji (m)	[miʃ cénɟi]
beef	mish lope (m)	[miʃ lópɛ]
rabbit	mish lepuri (m)	[miʃ lépuri]

sausage (bologna, etc.)	salsiçe (f)	[salsítʃɛ]
vienna sausage (frankfurter)	salsiçe vjeneze (f)	[salsítʃɛ vjɛnézɛ]
bacon	proshutë (f)	[proʃútə]
ham	sallam (m)	[saɫám]
gammon	kofshë derri (f)	[kófʃə déri]

pâté	pate (f)	[paté]
liver	mëlçi (f)	[məltʃí]
hamburger (ground beef)	hamburger (m)	[hamburgér]
tongue	gjuhë (f)	[ɟúhə]

egg	ve (f)	[vɛ]
eggs	vezë (pl)	[vézə]
egg white	e bardhë veze (f)	[ɛ bárðə vézɛ]
egg yolk	e verdhë veze (f)	[ɛ vérðə vézɛ]

fish	peshk (m)	[pɛʃk]
seafood	fruta deti (pl)	[frúta déti]
crustaceans	krustace (pl)	[krustátsɛ]
caviar	havjar (m)	[havjár]

crab	gaforre (f)	[gafórɛ]
shrimp	karkalec (m)	[karkaléts]
oyster	midhje (f)	[míðjɛ]
spiny lobster	karavidhe (f)	[karavíðɛ]
octopus	oktapod (m)	[oktapód]
squid	kallamarë (f)	[kaɫamárə]

sturgeon	bli (m)	[blí]
salmon	salmon (m)	[salmón]
halibut	shojzë e Atlantikut Verior (f)	[ʃójzə ɛ atlantíkut vɛriór]

cod	merluc (m)	[mɛrlúts]
mackerel	skumbri (m)	[skúmbri]
tuna	tunë (f)	[túnə]
eel	ngjalë (f)	[nɟálə]

trout	troftë (f)	[tróftə]
sardine	sardele (f)	[sardélɛ]
pike	mlysh (m)	[mlýʃ]

herring	harengë (f)	[harénjə]
bread	bukë (f)	[búkə]
cheese	djath (m)	[djáθ]
sugar	sheqer (m)	[ʃɛcér]
salt	kripë (f)	[krípə]

rice	oriz (m)	[oríz]
pasta (macaroni)	makarona (f)	[makaróna]
noodles	makarona petë (f)	[makaróna pétə]

butter	gjalp (m)	[ɟalp]
vegetable oil	vaj vegjetal (m)	[vaj vɛɟɛtál]
sunflower oil	vaj luledielli (m)	[vaj lulɛdiéɬi]
margarine	margarinë (f)	[margarínə]

| olives | ullinj (pl) | [uɬíɲ] |
| olive oil | vaj ulliri (m) | [vaj uɬíri] |

milk	qumësht (m)	[cúməʃt]
condensed milk	qumësht i kondensuar (m)	[cúməʃt i kondɛnsúar]
yogurt	kos (m)	[kos]
sour cream	salcë kosi (f)	[sáltsə kosi]
cream (of milk)	krem qumështi (m)	[krɛm cúməʃti]

| mayonnaise | majonezë (f) | [majonézə] |
| buttercream | krem gjalpi (m) | [krɛm ɟálpi] |

groats (barley ~, etc.)	drithëra (pl)	[dríθəra]
flour	miell (m)	[míɛɬ]
canned food	konserva (f)	[konsérva]

cornflakes	kornfleiks (m)	[kornfléiks]
honey	mjaltë (f)	[mjáltə]
jam	reçel (m)	[rɛtʃél]
chewing gum	çamçakëz (m)	[tʃamtʃakéz]

53. Drinks

water	ujë (m)	[újə]
drinking water	ujë i pijshëm (m)	[újə i píjʃəm]
mineral water	ujë mineral (m)	[újə minɛrál]

still (adj)	ujë natyral	[újə natyrál]
carbonated (adj)	ujë i karbonuar	[újə i karbonúar]
sparkling (adj)	ujë i gazuar	[újə i gazúar]
ice	akull (m)	[ákuɬ]
with ice	me akull	[mɛ ákuɬ]

| non-alcoholic (adj) | jo alkoolik | [jo alkoolík] |
| soft drink | pije e lehtë (f) | [píjɛ ɛ léhtə] |

| refreshing drink | pije freskuese (f) | [píjɛ frɛskúɛsɛ] |
| lemonade | limonadë (f) | [limonádə] |

liquors	likere (pl)	[likérɛ]
wine	verë (f)	[vérə]
white wine	verë e bardhë (f)	[vérə ɛ bárðə]
red wine	verë e kuqe (f)	[vérə ɛ kúcɛ]

liqueur	liker (m)	[likér]
champagne	shampanjë (f)	[ʃampáɲə]
vermouth	vermut (m)	[vɛrmút]

whiskey	uiski (m)	[víski]
vodka	vodkë (f)	[vódkə]
gin	xhin (m)	[dʒin]
cognac	konjak (m)	[koɲák]
rum	rum (m)	[rum]

coffee	kafe (f)	[káfɛ]
black coffee	kafe e zezë (f)	[káfɛ ɛ zézə]
coffee with milk	kafe me qumësht (m)	[káfɛ mɛ cúməʃt]
cappuccino	kapuçino (m)	[kaputʃíno]
instant coffee	neskafe (f)	[nɛskáfɛ]

milk	qumësht (m)	[cúməʃt]
cocktail	koktej (m)	[koktéj]
milkshake	milkshake (f)	[milkʃákɛ]

juice	lëng frutash (m)	[ləŋ frútaʃ]
tomato juice	lëng domatesh (m)	[ləŋ domátɛʃ]
orange juice	lëng portokalli (m)	[ləŋ portokáɬi]
freshly squeezed juice	lëng frutash i freskët (m)	[ləŋ frútaʃ i fréskət]

beer	birrë (f)	[bírə]
light beer	birrë e lehtë (f)	[bírə ɛ léhtə]
dark beer	birrë e zezë (f)	[bírə ɛ zézə]

tea	çaj (m)	[tʃáj]
black tea	çaj i zi (m)	[tʃáj i zí]
green tea	çaj jeshil (m)	[tʃáj jɛʃíl]

54. Vegetables

| vegetables | perime (pl) | [pɛrímɛ] |
| greens | zarzavate (pl) | [zarzavátɛ] |

tomato	domate (f)	[domátɛ]
cucumber	kastravec (m)	[kastravéts]
carrot	karotë (f)	[karótə]
potato	patate (f)	[patátɛ]

| onion | qepë (f) | [cépə] |
| garlic | hudhër (f) | [húðər] |

cabbage	lakër (f)	[lákər]
cauliflower	lulelakër (f)	[lulɛlákər]
Brussels sprouts	lakër Brukseli (f)	[lákər brukséli]
broccoli	brokoli (m)	[brókoli]

beet	panxhar (m)	[pandʒár]
eggplant	patëllxhan (m)	[patəɫdʒán]
zucchini	kungulleshë (m)	[kuŋuɫéʃə]
pumpkin	kungull (m)	[kúŋuɫ]
turnip	rrepë (f)	[répə]

parsley	majdanoz (m)	[majdanóz]
dill	kopër (f)	[kópər]
lettuce	sallatë jeshile (f)	[saɫátə jɛʃílɛ]
celery	selino (f)	[sɛlíno]
asparagus	asparagus (m)	[asparágus]
spinach	spinaq (m)	[spinác]

pea	bizele (f)	[bizélɛ]
beans	fasule (f)	[fasúlɛ]
corn (maize)	misër (m)	[mísər]
kidney bean	groshë (f)	[gróʃə]

bell pepper	spec (m)	[spɛts]
radish	rrepkë (f)	[répkə]
artichoke	angjinare (f)	[aɲináɾɛ]

55. Fruits. Nuts

fruit	frut (m)	[frut]
apple	mollë (f)	[móɫə]
pear	dardhë (f)	[dárðə]
lemon	limon (m)	[limón]
orange	portokall (m)	[portokáɫ]
strawberry (garden ~)	luleshtrydhe (f)	[lulɛʃtrýðɛ]

mandarin	mandarinë (f)	[mandarínə]
plum	kumbull (f)	[kúmbuɫ]
peach	pjeshkë (f)	[pjéʃkə]
apricot	kajsi (f)	[kajsí]
raspberry	mjedër (f)	[mjédər]
pineapple	ananas (m)	[ananás]

banana	banane (f)	[banánɛ]
watermelon	shalqi (m)	[ʃalcí]
grape	rrush (m)	[ruʃ]
sour cherry	qershi vishnje (f)	[cɛrʃí víʃɲɛ]

| sweet cherry | qershi (f) | [cɛrʃí] |
| melon | pjepër (m) | [pjépər] |

grapefruit	grejpfrut (m)	[grɛjpfrút]
avocado	avokado (f)	[avokádo]
papaya	papaja (f)	[papája]
mango	mango (f)	[máŋo]
pomegranate	shegë (f)	[ʃégə]

redcurrant	kaliboba e kuqe (f)	[kalibóba ɛ kúcɛ]
blackcurrant	kaliboba e zezë (f)	[kalibóba ɛ zézə]
gooseberry	kulumbri (f)	[kulumbrí]
bilberry	boronicë (f)	[boronítsə]
blackberry	manaferra (f)	[manaféra]

raisin	rrush i thatë (m)	[ruʃ i θátə]
fig	fik (m)	[fik]
date	hurmë (f)	[húrmə]

peanut	kikirik (m)	[kikirík]
almond	bajame (f)	[bajámɛ]
walnut	arrë (f)	[árə]
hazelnut	lajthi (f)	[lajθí]
coconut	arrë kokosi (f)	[árə kokósi]
pistachios	fëstëk (m)	[fəstə́k]

56. Bread. Candy

bakers' confectionery (pastry)	ëmbëlsira (pl)	[əmbəlsíra]
bread	bukë (f)	[búkə]
cookies	biskota (pl)	[biskóta]

chocolate (n)	çokollatë (f)	[tʃokołátə]
chocolate (as adj)	prej çokollate	[prɛj tʃokołátɛ]
candy (wrapped)	karamele (f)	[karamélɛ]

| cake (e.g., cupcake) | kek (m) | [kék] |
| cake (e.g., birthday ~) | tortë (f) | [tórtə] |

| pie (e.g., apple ~) | tortë (f) | [tórtə] |
| filling (for cake, pie) | mbushje (f) | [mbúʃɛ] |

| jam (whole fruit jam) | reçel (m) | [rɛtʃél] |
| marmalade | marmelatë (f) | [marmɛlátə] |

wafers	vafera (pl)	[vaféra]
ice-cream	akullore (f)	[akułórɛ]
pudding	puding (m)	[pudíŋ]

57. Spices

salt	**kripë** (f)	[krípə]
salty (adj)	**i kripur**	[i krípur]
to salt (vt)	**hedh kripë**	[hɛð krípə]
black pepper	**piper i zi** (m)	[pipér i zi]
red pepper (milled ~)	**piper i kuq** (m)	[pipér i kuc]
mustard	**mustardë** (f)	[mustárdə]
horseradish	**rrepë djegëse** (f)	[répə djégəsɛ]
condiment	**salcë** (f)	[sáltsə]
spice	**erëz** (f)	[érəz]
sauce	**salcë** (f)	[sáltsə]
vinegar	**uthull** (f)	[úθuɫ]
anise	**anisetë** (f)	[anisétə]
basil	**borzilok** (m)	[borzilók]
cloves	**karafil** (m)	[karafíl]
ginger	**xhenxhefil** (m)	[dʒɛndʒɛfíl]
coriander	**koriandër** (m)	[koriándər]
cinnamon	**kanellë** (f)	[kanéɫə]
sesame	**susam** (m)	[susám]
bay leaf	**gjeth dafine** (m)	[ɟɛθ dafínɛ]
paprika	**spec** (m)	[spɛts]
caraway	**kumin** (m)	[kumín]
saffron	**shafran** (m)	[ʃafrán]

PERSONAL INFORMATION. FAMILY

58. Personal information. Forms

name (first name)	**emër** (m)	[émər]
surname (last name)	**mbiemër** (m)	[mbiémər]
date of birth	**datëlindje** (f)	[datəlíndjɛ]
place of birth	**vendlindje** (f)	[vɛndlíndjɛ]
nationality	**kombësi** (f)	[kombəsí]
place of residence	**vendbanim** (m)	[vɛndbaním]
country	**shtet** (m)	[ʃtɛt]
profession (occupation)	**profesion** (m)	[profɛsión]
gender, sex	**gjinia** (f)	[ɟinía]
height	**gjatësia** (f)	[ɟatəsía]
weight	**peshë** (f)	[péʃə]

59. Family members. Relatives

mother	**nënë** (f)	[nénə]
father	**baba** (f)	[babá]
son	**bir** (m)	[bir]
daughter	**bijë** (f)	[bíjə]
younger daughter	**vajza e vogël** (f)	[vájza ɛ vógəl]
younger son	**djali i vogël** (m)	[djáli i vógəl]
eldest daughter	**vajza e madhe** (f)	[vájza ɛ máðɛ]
eldest son	**djali i vogël** (m)	[djáli i vógəl]
brother	**vëlla** (m)	[vəłá]
elder brother	**vëllai i madh** (m)	[vəłái i mað]
younger brother	**vëllai i vogël** (m)	[vəłai i vógəl]
sister	**motër** (f)	[mótər]
elder sister	**motra e madhe** (f)	[mótra ɛ máðɛ]
younger sister	**motra e vogël** (f)	[mótra ɛ vógəl]
cousin (masc.)	**kushëri** (m)	[kuʃərí]
cousin (fem.)	**kushërirë** (f)	[kuʃərírə]
mom, mommy	**mami** (f)	[mámi]
dad, daddy	**babi** (m)	[bábi]
parents	**prindër** (pl)	[príndər]
child	**fëmijë** (f)	[fəmíjə]

children	**fëmijë** (pl)	[fəmíjə]
grandmother	**gjyshe** (f)	[ɟýʃɛ]
grandfather	**gjysh** (m)	[ɟyʃ]
grandson	**nip** (m)	[nip]
granddaughter	**mbesë** (f)	[mbésə]
grandchildren	**nipër e mbesa** (pl)	[nípər ɛ mbésa]
uncle	**dajë** (f)	[dájə]
aunt	**teze** (f)	[tézɛ]
nephew	**nip** (m)	[nip]
niece	**mbesë** (f)	[mbésə]
mother-in-law (wife's mother)	**vjehrrë** (f)	[vjéhrə]
father-in-law (husband's father)	**vjehrri** (m)	[vjéhri]
son-in-law (daughter's husband)	**dhëndër** (m)	[ðéndər]
stepmother	**njerkë** (f)	[ɲérkə]
stepfather	**njerk** (m)	[ɲérk]
infant	**foshnjë** (f)	[fóʃnə]
baby (infant)	**fëmijë** (f)	[fəmíjə]
little boy, kid	**djalosh** (m)	[djalóʃ]
wife	**bashkëshorte** (f)	[baʃkəʃórtɛ]
husband	**bashkëshort** (m)	[baʃkəʃórt]
spouse (husband)	**bashkëshort** (m)	[baʃkəʃórt]
spouse (wife)	**bashkëshorte** (f)	[baʃkəʃórtɛ]
married (masc.)	**i martuar**	[i martúar]
married (fem.)	**e martuar**	[ɛ martúar]
single (unmarried)	**beqar**	[bɛcár]
bachelor	**beqar** (m)	[bɛcár]
divorced (masc.)	**i divorcuar**	[i divortsúar]
widow	**vejushë** (f)	[vɛjúʃə]
widower	**vejan** (m)	[vɛján]
relative	**kushëri** (m)	[kuʃərí]
close relative	**kushëri i afërt** (m)	[kuʃərí i áfərt]
distant relative	**kushëri i largët** (m)	[kuʃərí i lárgət]
relatives	**kushërinj** (pl)	[kuʃəríɲ]
orphan (boy)	**jetim** (m)	[jɛtím]
orphan (girl)	**jetime** (f)	[jɛtímɛ]
guardian (of a minor)	**kujdestar** (m)	[kujdɛstár]
to adopt (a boy)	**adoptoj**	[adoptój]
to adopt (a girl)	**adoptoj**	[adoptój]

60. Friends. Coworkers

friend (masc.)	**mik** (m)	[mik]
friend (fem.)	**mike** (f)	[míkɛ]
friendship	**miqësi** (f)	[micəsí]
to be friends	**të miqësohem**	[tə micəsóhɛm]
buddy (masc.)	**shok** (m)	[ʃok]
buddy (fem.)	**shoqe** (f)	[ʃócɛ]
partner	**partner** (m)	[partnér]
chief (boss)	**shef** (m)	[ʃɛf]
superior (n)	**epror** (m)	[ɛprór]
owner, proprietor	**pronar** (m)	[pronár]
subordinate (n)	**vartës** (m)	[vártəs]
colleague	**koleg** (m)	[kolég]
acquaintance (person)	**i njohur** (m)	[i ɲóhur]
fellow traveler	**bashkudhëtar** (m)	[baʃkuðətár]
classmate	**shok klase** (m)	[ʃok klásɛ]
neighbor (masc.)	**komshi** (m)	[komʃí]
neighbor (fem.)	**komshike** (f)	[komʃíkɛ]
neighbors	**komshinj** (pl)	[komʃíɲ]

HUMAN BODY. MEDICINE

61. Head

head	**kokë** (f)	[kókə]
face	**fytyrë** (f)	[fytýrə]
nose	**hundë** (f)	[húndə]
mouth	**gojë** (f)	[gójə]
eye	**sy** (m)	[sy]
eyes	**sytë**	[sýtə]
pupil	**bebëz** (f)	[bébəz]
eyebrow	**vetull** (f)	[vétuɫ]
eyelash	**qerpik** (m)	[cɛrpík]
eyelid	**qepallë** (f)	[cɛpáɫə]
tongue	**gjuhë** (f)	[ɟúhə]
tooth	**dhëmb** (m)	[ðəmb]
lips	**buzë** (f)	[búzə]
cheekbones	**mollëza** (f)	[móɫəza]
gum	**mishrat e dhëmbëve**	[míʃrat ɛ ðəmbəvɛ]
palate	**qiellzë** (f)	[ciéɫzə]
nostrils	**vrimat e hundës** (pl)	[vrímat ɛ húndəs]
chin	**mjekër** (f)	[mjékər]
jaw	**nofull** (f)	[nófuɫ]
cheek	**faqe** (f)	[fácɛ]
forehead	**ball** (m)	[báɫ]
temple	**tëmth** (m)	[təmθ]
ear	**vesh** (m)	[vɛʃ]
back of the head	**zverk** (m)	[zvɛrk]
neck	**qafë** (f)	[cáfə]
throat	**fyt** (m)	[fyt]
hair	**flokë** (pl)	[flókə]
hairstyle	**model flokësh** (m)	[modél flókəʃ]
haircut	**prerje flokësh** (f)	[prérjɛ flókəʃ]
wig	**paruke** (f)	[parúkɛ]
mustache	**mustaqe** (f)	[mustácɛ]
beard	**mjekër** (f)	[mjékər]
to have (a beard, etc.)	**lë mjekër**	[lə mjékər]
braid	**gërshet** (m)	[gərʃét]
sideburns	**baseta** (f)	[baséta]
red-haired (adj)	**flokëkuqe**	[flokəkúcɛ]

gray (hair)	**thinja**	[θíɲa]
bald (adj)	**qeros**	[cɛrós]
bald patch	**tullë** (f)	[túɫə]

| ponytail | **bishtalec** (m) | [biʃtaléts] |
| bangs | **balluke** (f) | [baɫúkɛ] |

62. Human body

| hand | **dorë** (f) | [dórə] |
| arm | **krah** (m) | [krah] |

finger	**gisht i dorës** (m)	[gíʃt i dórəs]
toe	**gisht i këmbës** (m)	[gíʃt i kémbəs]
thumb	**gishti i madh** (m)	[gíʃti i máð]
little finger	**gishti i vogël** (m)	[gíʃti i vógəl]
nail	**thua** (f)	[θúa]

fist	**grusht** (m)	[grúʃt]
palm	**pëllëmbë dore** (f)	[pəɫémbə dórɛ]
wrist	**kyç** (m)	[kytʃ]
forearm	**parakrah** (m)	[parakráh]
elbow	**bërryl** (m)	[bərýl]
shoulder	**shpatull** (f)	[ʃpátuɫ]

leg	**këmbë** (f)	[kémbə]
foot	**shputë** (f)	[ʃpútə]
knee	**gju** (m)	[ɟú]
calf (part of leg)	**pulpë** (f)	[púlpə]
hip	**ijë** (f)	[íjə]
heel	**thembër** (f)	[θémbər]

body	**trup** (m)	[trup]
stomach	**stomak** (m)	[stomák]
chest	**kraharor** (m)	[kraharór]
breast	**gjoks** (m)	[ɟóks]
flank	**krah** (m)	[krah]
back	**kurriz** (m)	[kuríz]
lower back	**fundshpina** (f)	[fundʃpína]
waist	**beli** (m)	[béli]

navel (belly button)	**kërthizë** (f)	[kərθízə]
buttocks	**vithe** (f)	[víθɛ]
bottom	**prapanica** (f)	[prapanítsa]

beauty mark	**nishan** (m)	[niʃán]
birthmark (café au lait spot)	**shenjë lindjeje** (f)	[ʃéɲə líndjɛjɛ]
tattoo	**tatuazh** (m)	[tatuáʒ]
scar	**shenjë** (f)	[ʃéɲə]

63. Diseases

sickness	sëmundje (f)	[səmúndjɛ]
to be sick	jam sëmurë	[jam səmúrə]
health	shëndet (m)	[ʃəndét]
runny nose (coryza)	rrifë (f)	[rífə]
tonsillitis	grykët (m)	[grýkət]
cold (illness)	ftohje (f)	[ftóhjɛ]
to catch a cold	ftohem	[ftóhɛm]
bronchitis	bronkit (m)	[bronkít]
pneumonia	pneumoni (f)	[pnɛumoní]
flu, influenza	grip (m)	[grip]
nearsighted (adj)	miop	[mióp]
farsighted (adj)	presbit	[prɛsbít]
strabismus (crossed eyes)	strabizëm (m)	[strabízəm]
cross-eyed (adj)	strabik	[strabík]
cataract	katarakt (m)	[katarákt]
glaucoma	glaukoma (f)	[glaukóma]
stroke	goditje (f)	[godítjɛ]
heart attack	sulm në zemër (m)	[sulm nə zémər]
myocardial infarction	infarkt miokardiak (m)	[infárkt miokardiák]
paralysis	paralizë (f)	[paralízə]
to paralyze (vt)	paralizoj	[paralizój]
allergy	alergji (f)	[alɛɟí]
asthma	astmë (f)	[ástmə]
diabetes	diabet (m)	[diabét]
toothache	dhimbje dhëmbi (f)	[ðímbjɛ ðə́mbi]
caries	karies (m)	[kariés]
diarrhea	diarre (f)	[diaré]
constipation	kapsllëk (m)	[kapsɫə́k]
stomach upset	dispepsi (f)	[dispɛpsí]
food poisoning	helmim (m)	[hɛlmím]
to get food poisoning	helmohem nga ushqimi	[hɛlmóhɛm ŋa uʃcími]
arthritis	artrit (m)	[artrít]
rickets	rakit (m)	[rakít]
rheumatism	reumatizëm (m)	[rɛumatízəm]
atherosclerosis	arteriosklerozë (f)	[artɛriosklɛrózə]
gastritis	gastrit (m)	[gastrít]
appendicitis	apendicit (m)	[apɛnditsít]
cholecystitis	kolecistit (m)	[kolɛtsistít]
ulcer	ulcerë (f)	[ultsérə]
measles	fruth (m)	[fruθ]

rubella (German measles)	rubeola (f)	[rubɛóla]
jaundice	verdhëza (f)	[vérðəza]
hepatitis	hepatit (m)	[hɛpatít]

schizophrenia	skizofreni (f)	[skizofrɛní]
rabies (hydrophobia)	sëmundje e tërbimit (f)	[səmúndjɛ ɛ tərbímit]
neurosis	neurozë (f)	[nɛurózə]
concussion	tronditje (f)	[trondítjɛ]

cancer	kancer (m)	[kantsér]
sclerosis	sklerozë (f)	[sklɛrózə]
multiple sclerosis	sklerozë e shumëfishtë (f)	[sklɛrózə ɛ ʃuməfíʃtə]

alcoholism	alkoolizëm (m)	[alkoolízəm]
alcoholic (n)	alkoolik (m)	[alkoolík]
syphilis	sifiliz (m)	[sifilíz]
AIDS	SIDA (f)	[sída]

tumor	tumor (m)	[tumór]
malignant (adj)	malinj	[malíɲ]
benign (adj)	beninj	[bɛníɲ]

fever	ethe (f)	[éθɛ]
malaria	malarie (f)	[malaríɛ]
gangrene	gangrenë (f)	[gaɲrénə]
seasickness	sëmundje deti (f)	[səmúndjɛ déti]
epilepsy	epilepsi (f)	[ɛpilɛpsí]

epidemic	epidemi (f)	[ɛpidɛmí]
typhus	tifo (f)	[tífo]
tuberculosis	tuberkuloz (f)	[tubɛrkulóz]
cholera	kolerë (f)	[kolérə]
plague (bubonic ~)	murtaja (f)	[murtája]

64. Symptoms. Treatments. Part 1

symptom	simptomë (f)	[simptómə]
temperature	temperaturë (f)	[tɛmpɛratúrə]
high temperature (fever)	temperaturë e lartë (f)	[tɛmpɛratúrə ɛ lártə]
pulse (heartbeat)	puls (m)	[puls]

dizziness (vertigo)	marrje mendsh (m)	[márjɛ méndʃ]
hot (adj)	i nxehtë	[i ndzéhtə]
shivering	drithërima (f)	[driθəríma]
pale (e.g., ~ face)	i zbehur	[i zbéhur]

cough	kollë (f)	[kótə]
to cough (vi)	kollitem	[kołítɛm]
to sneeze (vi)	teshtij	[tɛʃtíj]
faint	të fikët (f)	[tə fíkət]

to faint (vi)	bie të fikët	[bíɛ tə fíkət]
bruise (hématome)	mavijosje (f)	[mavijósjɛ]
bump (lump)	gungë (f)	[gúŋə]
to bang (bump)	godas	[godás]
contusion (bruise)	lëndim (m)	[ləndím]
to get a bruise	lëndohem	[ləndóhɛm]

to limp (vi)	çaloj	[tʃalój]
dislocation	dislokim (m)	[dislokím]
to dislocate (vt)	del nga vendi	[dɛl ŋa véndi]
fracture	thyerje (f)	[θýɛrjɛ]
to have a fracture	thyej	[θýɛj]

cut (e.g., paper ~)	e prerë (f)	[ɛ prérə]
to cut oneself	pres veten	[prɛs vétɛn]
bleeding	rrjedhje gjaku (f)	[rjéðjɛ ɟáku]

| burn (injury) | djegie (f) | [djégiɛ] |
| to get burned | digjem | [díɟɛm] |

to prick (vt)	shpoj	[ʃpoj]
to prick oneself	shpohem	[ʃpóhɛm]
to injure (vt)	dëmtoj	[dəmtój]
injury	dëmtim (m)	[dəmtím]
wound	plagë (f)	[plágə]
trauma	traumë (f)	[traúmə]

to be delirious	fol përçart	[fól pərtʃárt]
to stutter (vi)	belbëzoj	[bɛlbəzój]
sunstroke	pikë e diellit (f)	[píkə ɛ diéłit]

65. Symptoms. Treatments. Part 2

| pain, ache | dhimbje (f) | [ðímbjɛ] |
| splinter (in foot, etc.) | cifël (f) | [tsífəl] |

sweat (perspiration)	djersë (f)	[djérsə]
to sweat (perspire)	djersij	[djɛrsíj]
vomiting	të vjella (f)	[tə vjéła]
convulsions	konvulsione (f)	[konvulsiónɛ]

pregnant (adj)	shtatzënë	[ʃtatzénə]
to be born	lind	[lind]
delivery, labor	lindje (f)	[líndjɛ]
to deliver (~ a baby)	sjell në jetë	[sjɛɫ nə jétə]
abortion	abort (m)	[abórt]

breathing, respiration	frymëmarrje (f)	[fryməmárjɛ]
in-breath (inhalation)	mbajtje e frymës (f)	[mbájtjɛ ɛ frýməs]
out-breath (exhalation)	lëshim i frymës (m)	[ləʃím i frýməs]

to exhale (breathe out)	nxjerr frymën	[ndzjér frýmən]
to inhale (vi)	marr frymë	[mar frýmə]
disabled person	invalid (m)	[invalíd]
cripple	i gjymtuar (m)	[i ɟymtúar]
drug addict	narkoman (m)	[narkomán]
deaf (adj)	shurdh	[ʃurð]
mute (adj)	memec	[mɛméts]
deaf mute (adj)	shurdh-memec	[ʃurð-mɛméts]
mad, insane (adj)	i marrë	[i márə]
madman (demented person)	i çmendur (m)	[i tʃméndur]
madwoman	e çmendur (f)	[ɛ tʃméndur]
to go insane	çmendem	[tʃméndɛm]
gene	gen (m)	[gɛn]
immunity	imunitet (m)	[imunitét]
hereditary (adj)	e trashëguar	[ɛ traʃəgúar]
congenital (adj)	e lindur	[ɛ líndur]
virus	virus (m)	[virús]
microbe	mikrob (m)	[mikrób]
bacterium	bakterie (f)	[baktériɛ]
infection	infeksion (m)	[infɛksión]

66. Symptoms. Treatments. Part 3

hospital	spital (m)	[spitál]
patient	pacient (m)	[patsiént]
diagnosis	diagnozë (f)	[diagnózə]
cure	kurë (f)	[kúrə]
medical treatment	trajtim mjekësor (m)	[trajtím mjɛkəsór]
to get treatment	kurohem	[kuróhɛm]
to treat (~ a patient)	kuroj	[kurój]
to nurse (look after)	kujdesem	[kujdésɛm]
care (nursing ~)	kujdes (m)	[kujdés]
operation, surgery	operacion (m)	[opɛratsión]
to bandage (head, limb)	fashoj	[faʃój]
bandaging	fashim (m)	[faʃím]
vaccination	vaksinim (m)	[vaksiním]
to vaccinate (vt)	vaksinoj	[vaksinój]
injection, shot	injeksion (m)	[iɲɛksión]
to give an injection	bëj injeksion	[bəj iɲɛksíon]
attack	atak (m)	[aták]
amputation	amputim (m)	[amputím]

to amputate (vt)	**amputoj**	[amputój]
coma	**komë** (f)	[kómə]
to be in a coma	**jam në komë**	[jam nə kómə]
intensive care	**kujdes intensiv** (m)	[kujdés intɛnsív]
to recover (~ from flu)	**shërohem**	[ʃəróhɛm]
condition (patient's ~)	**gjendje** (f)	[ɟéndjɛ]
consciousness	**vetëdije** (f)	[vɛtədíjɛ]
memory (faculty)	**kujtesë** (f)	[kujtésə]
to pull out (tooth)	**heq**	[hɛc]
filling	**mbushje** (f)	[mbúʃjɛ]
to fill (a tooth)	**mbush**	[mbúʃ]
hypnosis	**hipnozë** (f)	[hipnózə]
to hypnotize (vt)	**hipnotizim**	[hipnotizím]

67. Medicine. Drugs. Accessories

medicine, drug	**ilaç** (m)	[ilátʃ]
remedy	**mjekim** (m)	[mjɛkím]
to prescribe (vt)	**shkruaj recetë**	[ʃkrúaj rɛtsétə]
prescription	**recetë** (f)	[rɛtsétə]
tablet, pill	**pilulë** (f)	[pilúlə]
ointment	**krem** (m)	[krɛm]
ampule	**ampulë** (f)	[ampúlə]
mixture, solution	**përzierje** (f)	[pərzíɛrjɛ]
syrup	**shurup** (m)	[ʃurúp]
capsule	**pilulë** (f)	[pilúlə]
powder	**pudër** (f)	[púdər]
gauze bandage	**fashë garze** (f)	[faʃə gárzɛ]
cotton wool	**pambuk** (m)	[pambúk]
iodine	**jod** (m)	[jod]
Band-Aid	**leukoplast** (m)	[lɛukoplást]
eyedropper	**pikatore** (f)	[pikatórɛ]
thermometer	**termometër** (m)	[tɛrmométər]
syringe	**shiringë** (f)	[ʃiríŋə]
wheelchair	**karrocë me rrota** (f)	[karótsə mɛ róta]
crutches	**paterica** (f)	[patɛrítsa]
painkiller	**qetësues** (m)	[cɛtəsúɛs]
laxative	**laksativ** (m)	[laksatív]
spirits (ethanol)	**alkool dezinfektues** (m)	[alkoól dɛzinfɛktúɛs]
medicinal herbs	**bimë mjekësore** (f)	[bímə mjɛkəsórɛ]
herbal (~ tea)	**çaj bimor**	[tʃáj bimór]

APARTMENT

68. Apartment

apartment	apartament (m)	[apartamént]
room	dhomë (f)	[ðómə]
bedroom	dhomë gjumi (f)	[ðómə ɟúmi]
dining room	dhomë ngrënie (f)	[ðómə ŋrəníɛ]
living room	dhomë ndeje (f)	[ðómə ndéjɛ]
study (home office)	dhomë pune (f)	[ðómə púnɛ]
entry room	hyrje (f)	[hýrjɛ]
bathroom (room with a bath or shower)	banjo (f)	[báɲo]
half bath	tualet (m)	[tualét]
ceiling	tavan (m)	[taván]
floor	dysheme (f)	[dyʃɛmé]
corner	qoshe (f)	[cóʃɛ]

69. Furniture. Interior

furniture	orendi (f)	[orɛndí]
table	tryezë (f)	[tryézə]
chair	karrige (f)	[karígɛ]
bed	shtrat (m)	[ʃtrat]
couch, sofa	divan (m)	[diván]
armchair	kolltuk (m)	[koɬtúk]
bookcase	raft librash (m)	[ráft líbraʃ]
shelf	sergjen (m)	[sɛrɟén]
wardrobe	gardërobë (f)	[gardəróbə]
coat rack (wall-mounted ~)	varëse (f)	[várəsɛ]
coat stand	varëse xhaketash (f)	[várəsɛ dʒakétaʃ]
bureau, dresser	komodë (f)	[komódə]
coffee table	tryezë e ulët (f)	[tryézə ɛ úlət]
mirror	pasqyrë (f)	[pascýrə]
carpet	qilim (m)	[cilím]
rug, small carpet	tapet (m)	[tapét]
fireplace	oxhak (m)	[odʒák]
candle	qiri (m)	[círi]

candlestick	shandan (m)	[ʃandán]
drapes	perde (f)	[pérdɛ]
wallpaper	tapiceri (f)	[tapitsɛrí]
blinds (jalousie)	grila (f)	[gríla]

table lamp	llambë tavoline (f)	[ɫámbə tavolínɛ]
wall lamp (sconce)	llambadar muri (m)	[ɫambadár múri]
floor lamp	llambadar (m)	[ɫambadár]
chandelier	llambadar (m)	[ɫambadár]

leg (of chair, table)	këmbë (f)	[kémbə]
armrest	mbështetëse krahu (f)	[mbəʃtétəsɛ kráhu]
back (backrest)	mbështetëse (f)	[mbəʃtétəsɛ]
drawer	sirtar (m)	[sirtár]

70. Bedding

bedclothes	çarçafë (pl)	[tʃartʃáfə]
pillow	jastëk (m)	[jasték]
pillowcase	këllëf jastëku (m)	[kəɫəf jastéku]
duvet, comforter	jorgan (m)	[jorgán]
sheet	çarçaf (m)	[tʃartʃáf]
bedspread	mbulesë (f)	[mbulésə]

71. Kitchen

kitchen	kuzhinë (f)	[kuʒínə]
gas	gaz (m)	[gaz]
gas stove (range)	sobë me gaz (f)	[sóbə mɛ gaz]
electric stove	sobë elektrike (f)	[sóbə ɛlɛktríkɛ]
oven	furrë (f)	[fúrə]
microwave oven	mikrovalë (f)	[mikrоválə]

refrigerator	frigorifer (m)	[frigorifér]
freezer	frigorifer (m)	[frigorifér]
dishwasher	pjatalarëse (f)	[pjatalárəsɛ]

meat grinder	grirëse mishi (f)	[grírəsɛ míʃi]
juicer	shtrydhëse frutash (f)	[ʃtrýðəsɛ frútaʃ]
toaster	toster (m)	[tostér]
mixer	mikser (m)	[miksér]

coffee machine	makinë kafeje (f)	[makínə kaféjɛ]
coffee pot	kafetierë (f)	[kafɛtiérə]
coffee grinder	mulli kafeje (f)	[muɫí káfɛjɛ]

| kettle | çajnik (m) | [tʃajník] |
| teapot | çajnik (m) | [tʃajník] |

| lid | kapak (m) | [kapák] |
| tea strainer | sitë çaji (f) | [sítə tʃáji] |

spoon	lugë (f)	[lúgə]
teaspoon	lugë çaji (f)	[lúgə tʃáji]
soup spoon	lugë gjelle (f)	[lúgə ɟétɛ]
fork	pirun (m)	[pirún]
knife	thikë (f)	[θíkə]

tableware (dishes)	enë kuzhine (f)	[énə kuʒínɛ]
plate (dinner ~)	pjatë (f)	[pjátə]
saucer	pjatë filxhani (f)	[pjátə fildʒáni]

shot glass	potir (m)	[potír]
glass (tumbler)	gotë (f)	[gótə]
cup	filxhan (m)	[fildʒán]

sugar bowl	tas për sheqer (m)	[tas pər ʃɛcér]
salt shaker	kripore (f)	[kripórɛ]
pepper shaker	enë piperi (f)	[énə pipéri]
butter dish	pjatë gjalpi (f)	[pjátə ɟálpi]

stock pot (soup pot)	tenxhere (f)	[tɛndʒérɛ]
frying pan (skillet)	tigan (m)	[tigán]
ladle	garuzhdë (f)	[garúʒdə]
colander	kullesë (f)	[kutésə]
tray (serving ~)	tabaka (f)	[tabaká]

bottle	shishe (f)	[ʃíʃɛ]
jar (glass)	kavanoz (m)	[kavanóz]
can	kanoçe (f)	[kanótʃɛ]

bottle opener	hapëse shishesh (f)	[hapəsé ʃíʃɛʃ]
can opener	hapëse kanoçesh (f)	[hapəsé kanótʃɛʃ]
corkscrew	turjelë tapash (f)	[turjélə tápaʃ]
filter	filtër (m)	[fíltər]
to filter (vt)	filtroj	[filtrój]

| trash, garbage (food waste, etc.) | pleh (m) | [plɛh] |
| trash can (kitchen ~) | kosh plehrash (m) | [koʃ pléhraʃ] |

72. Bathroom

bathroom	banjo (f)	[báɲo]
water	ujë (m)	[újə]
faucet	rubinet (m)	[rubinét]
hot water	ujë i nxehtë (f)	[újə i ndzéhtə]
cold water	ujë i ftohtë (f)	[újə i ftóhtə]
toothpaste	pastë dhëmbësh (f)	[pástə ðémbəʃ]

to brush one's teeth	laj dhëmbët	[laj ðémbət]
toothbrush	furçë dhëmbësh (f)	[fúrtʃə ðémbəʃ]
to shave (vi)	rruhem	[rúhɛm]
shaving foam	shkumë rroje (f)	[ʃkumə rójɛ]
razor	brisk (m)	[brísk]
to wash (one's hands, etc.)	laj duart	[laj dúart]
to take a bath	lahem	[láhɛm]
shower	dush (m)	[duʃ]
to take a shower	bëj dush	[bəj dúʃ]
bathtub	vaskë (f)	[váskə]
toilet (toilet bowl)	tualet (m)	[tualét]
sink (washbasin)	lavaman (m)	[lavamán]
soap	sapun (m)	[sapún]
soap dish	pjatë sapuni (f)	[pjátə sapúni]
sponge	sfungjer (m)	[sfunɟér]
shampoo	shampo (f)	[ʃampó]
towel	peshqir (m)	[pɛʃcír]
bathrobe	peshqir trupi (m)	[pɛʃcír trúpi]
laundry (laundering)	larje (f)	[lárjɛ]
washing machine	makinë larëse (f)	[makínə lárəsɛ]
to do the laundry	laj rroba	[laj róba]
laundry detergent	detergjent (m)	[dɛtɛɲént]

73. Household appliances

TV set	televizor (m)	[tɛlɛvizór]
tape recorder	inçizues me shirit (m)	[intʃizúɛs mɛ ʃirít]
VCR (video recorder)	video regjistrues (m)	[vídɛo rɛɟistrúɛs]
radio	radio (f)	[rádio]
player (CD, MP3, etc.)	kasetofon (m)	[kasɛtofón]
video projector	projektor (m)	[projɛktór]
home movie theater	kinema shtëpie (f)	[kinɛmá ʃtəpíɛ]
DVD player	DVD player (m)	[dividí plɛjər]
amplifier	amplifikator (m)	[amplifikatór]
video game console	konsol video loje (m)	[konsól vídɛo lójɛ]
video camera	videokamerë (f)	[vidɛokamérə]
camera (photo)	aparat fotografik (m)	[aparát fotografík]
digital camera	kamerë digjitale (f)	[kamérə diɟitálɛ]
vacuum cleaner	fshesë elektrike (f)	[fʃésə ɛlɛktríkɛ]
iron (e.g., steam ~)	hekur (m)	[hékur]
ironing board	tryezë për hekurosje (f)	[tryézə pər hɛkurósjɛ]

telephone	**telefon** (m)	[tɛlɛfón]
cell phone	**celular** (m)	[tsɛlulár]
typewriter	**makinë shkrimi** (f)	[makínə ʃkrími]
sewing machine	**makinë qepëse** (f)	[makínə cépəsɛ]

microphone	**mikrofon** (m)	[mikrofón]
headphones	**kufje** (f)	[kúfjɛ]
remote control (TV)	**telekomandë** (f)	[tɛlɛkomándə]

CD, compact disc	**CD** (f)	[tsɛdé]
cassette, tape	**kasetë** (f)	[kasétə]
vinyl record	**pllakë gramafoni** (f)	[pɫákə gramafóni]

THE EARTH. WEATHER

74. Outer space

space	**hapësirë** (f)	[hapəsírə]
space (as adj)	**hapësinor**	[hapəsinór]
outer space	**kozmos** (m)	[kozmós]
world	**botë** (f)	[bótə]
universe	**univers**	[univérs]
galaxy	**galaksi** (f)	[galaksí]
star	**yll** (m)	[yɫ]
constellation	**yllësi** (f)	[yɫəsí]
planet	**planet** (m)	[planét]
satellite	**satelit** (m)	[satɛlít]
meteorite	**meteor** (m)	[mɛtɛór]
comet	**kometë** (f)	[kométə]
asteroid	**asteroid** (m)	[astɛroíd]
orbit	**orbitë** (f)	[orbítə]
to revolve	**rrotullohet**	[rotuɫóhɛt]
(~ around the Earth)		
atmosphere	**atmosferë** (f)	[atmosférə]
the Sun	**Dielli** (m)	[diéɫi]
solar system	**sistemi diellor** (m)	[sistémi diɛɫór]
solar eclipse	**eklips diellor** (m)	[ɛklíps diɛɫór]
the Earth	**Toka** (f)	[tóka]
the Moon	**Hëna** (f)	[hə́na]
Mars	**Marsi** (m)	[mársi]
Venus	**Venera** (f)	[vɛnéra]
Jupiter	**Jupiteri** (m)	[jupitéri]
Saturn	**Saturni** (m)	[satúrni]
Mercury	**Merkuri** (m)	[mɛrkúri]
Uranus	**Urani** (m)	[uráni]
Neptune	**Neptuni** (m)	[nɛptúni]
Pluto	**Pluto** (f)	[plúto]
Milky Way	**Rruga e Qumështit** (f)	[rúga ɛ cúməʃtit]
Great Bear (Ursa Major)	**Arusha e Madhe** (f)	[arúʃa ɛ máðɛ]
North Star	**ylli i Veriut** (m)	[ýɫi i vériut]

Martian	Marsian (m)	[marsián]
extraterrestrial (n)	jashtëtokësor (m)	[jaʃtetokəsór]
alien	alien (m)	[alién]
flying saucer	disk fluturues (m)	[dísk fluturúɛs]

spaceship	anije kozmike (f)	[aníjɛ kozmíkɛ]
space station	stacion kozmik (m)	[statsión kozmík]
blast-off	ngritje (f)	[ŋrítjɛ]

engine	motor (m)	[motór]
nozzle	dizë (f)	[dízə]
fuel	karburant (m)	[karburánt]

cockpit, flight deck	kabinë pilotimi (f)	[kabínə pilotími]
antenna	antenë (f)	[anténə]
porthole	dritare anësore (f)	[dritárɛ anəsórɛ]
solar panel	panel solar (m)	[panél solár]
spacesuit	veshje astronauti (f)	[véʃjɛ astronáuti]

| weightlessness | mungesë graviteti (f) | [muŋésə gravitéti] |
| oxygen | oksigjen (m) | [oksiɟén] |

| docking (in space) | ndërlidhje në hapësirë (f) | [ndərlíðjɛ nə hapəsírə] |
| to dock (vi, vt) | stacionohem | [statsionóhɛm] |

observatory	observator (m)	[obsɛrvatór]
telescope	teleskop (m)	[tɛlɛskóp]
to observe (vt)	vëzhgoj	[vəʒgój]
to explore (vt)	eksploroj	[ɛksplorój]

75. The Earth

the Earth	Toka (f)	[tóka]
the globe (the Earth)	globi (f)	[glóbi]
planet	planet (m)	[planét]

atmosphere	atmosferë (f)	[atmosférə]
geography	gjeografi (f)	[ɟɛografí]
nature	natyrë (f)	[natýrə]

globe (table ~)	glob (m)	[glob]
map	hartë (f)	[hártə]
atlas	atlas (m)	[atlás]

Europe	Evropa (f)	[ɛvrópa]
Asia	Azia (f)	[azía]
Africa	Afrika (f)	[afríka]
Australia	Australia (f)	[australía]
America	Amerika (f)	[amɛríka]
North America	Amerika Veriore (f)	[amɛríka vɛriórɛ]

South America	**Amerika Jugore** (f)	[amɛríka jugórɛ]
Antarctica	**Antarktika** (f)	[antarktíka]
the Arctic	**Arktiku** (m)	[arktíku]

76. Cardinal directions

north	**veri** (m)	[vɛrí]
to the north	**drejt veriut**	[dréjt vériut]
in the north	**në veri**	[nə vɛrí]
northern (adj)	**verior**	[vɛriór]

south	**jug** (m)	[jug]
to the south	**drejt jugut**	[dréjt júgut]
in the south	**në jug**	[nə jug]
southern (adj)	**jugor**	[jugór]

west	**perëndim** (m)	[pɛrəndím]
to the west	**drejt perëndimit**	[dréjt pɛrəndímit]
in the west	**në perëndim**	[nə pɛrəndím]
western (adj)	**perëndimor**	[pɛrəndimór]

east	**lindje** (f)	[líndjɛ]
to the east	**drejt lindjes**	[dréjt líndjɛs]
in the east	**në lindje**	[nə líndjɛ]
eastern (adj)	**lindor**	[lindór]

77. Sea. Ocean

sea	**det** (m)	[dét]
ocean	**oqean** (m)	[ocɛán]
gulf (bay)	**gji** (m)	[ɟi]
straits	**ngushticë** (f)	[ŋuʃtítsə]

| land (solid ground) | **tokë** (f) | [tókə] |
| continent (mainland) | **kontinent** (m) | [kontinént] |

island	**ishull** (m)	[íʃuɫ]
peninsula	**gadishull** (m)	[gadíʃuɫ]
archipelago	**arkipelag** (m)	[arkipɛlág]

bay, cove	**gji** (m)	[ɟi]
harbor	**port** (m)	[port]
lagoon	**lagunë** (f)	[lagúnə]
cape	**kep** (m)	[kɛp]

atoll	**atol** (m)	[atól]
reef	**shkëmb nënujor** (m)	[ʃkəmb nənujór]
coral	**koral** (m)	[korál]

coral reef	korale nënujorë (f)	[korálɛ nənujórə]
deep (adj)	i thellë	[i θéɫə]
depth (deep water)	thellësi (f)	[θɛɫəsí]
abyss	humnerë (f)	[humnérə]
trench (e.g., Mariana ~)	hendek (m)	[hɛndék]

| current (Ocean ~) | rrymë (f) | [rýmə] |
| to surround (bathe) | rrethohet | [rɛθóhɛt] |

| shore | breg (m) | [brɛg] |
| coast | bregdet (m) | [brɛgdét] |

flow (flood tide)	batica (f)	[batítsa]
ebb (ebb tide)	zbaticë (f)	[zbatítsə]
shoal	cekëtinë (f)	[tsɛkətínə]
bottom (~ of the sea)	fund i detit (m)	[fúnd i détit]

wave	dallgë (f)	[dáɫgə]
crest (~ of a wave)	kreshtë (f)	[kréʃtə]
spume (sea foam)	shkumë (f)	[ʃkúmə]

storm (sea storm)	stuhi (f)	[stuhí]
hurricane	uragan (m)	[uragán]
tsunami	cunam (m)	[tsunám]
calm (dead ~)	qetësi (f)	[cɛtəsí]
quiet, calm (adj)	i qetë	[i cétə]

| pole | pol (m) | [pol] |
| polar (adj) | polar | [polár] |

latitude	gjerësi (f)	[ɟɛrəsí]
longitude	gjatësi (f)	[ɟatəsí]
parallel	paralele (f)	[paralélɛ]
equator	ekuator (m)	[ɛkuatór]

sky	qiell (m)	[cíɛɫ]
horizon	horizont (m)	[horizónt]
air	ajër (m)	[ájər]

lighthouse	fanar (m)	[fanár]
to dive (vi)	zhytem	[ʒýtɛm]
to sink (ab. boat)	fundosje	[fundósjɛ]
treasures	thesare (pl)	[θɛsárɛ]

78. Seas' and Oceans' names

Atlantic Ocean	Oqeani Atlantik (m)	[ocɛáni atlantík]
Indian Ocean	Oqeani Indian (m)	[ocɛáni indián]
Pacific Ocean	Oqeani Paqësor (m)	[ocɛáni pacəsór]
Arctic Ocean	Oqeani Arktik (m)	[ocɛáni arktík]

Black Sea	**Deti i Zi** (m)	[déti i zí]
Red Sea	**Deti i Kuq** (m)	[déti i kúc]
Yellow Sea	**Deti i Verdhë** (m)	[déti i vérðə]
White Sea	**Deti i Bardhë** (m)	[déti i bárðə]

Caspian Sea	**Deti Kaspik** (m)	[déti kaspík]
Dead Sea	**Deti i Vdekur** (m)	[déti i vdékuɾ]
Mediterranean Sea	**Deti Mesdhe** (m)	[déti mɛsðéj]

| Aegean Sea | **Deti Egje** (m) | [déti ɛɟé] |
| Adriatic Sea | **Deti Adriatik** (m) | [déti adriatík] |

Arabian Sea	**Deti Arab** (m)	[déti aráb]
Sea of Japan	**Deti i Japonisë** (m)	[déti i japonísə]
Bering Sea	**Deti Bering** (m)	[déti bériŋ]
South China Sea	**Deti i Kinës Jugore** (m)	[déti i kínəs jugóɾɛ]

Coral Sea	**Deti Koral** (m)	[déti korál]
Tasman Sea	**Deti Tasman** (m)	[déti tasmán]
Caribbean Sea	**Deti i Karaibeve** (m)	[déti i karaíbɛvɛ]

| Barents Sea | **Deti Barents** (m) | [déti barénts] |
| Kara Sea | **Deti Kara** (m) | [déti kára] |

North Sea	**Deti i Veriut** (m)	[déti i vériut]
Baltic Sea	**Deti Baltik** (m)	[déti baltík]
Norwegian Sea	**Deti Norvegjez** (m)	[déti noɾvɛɟéz]

79. Mountains

mountain	**mal** (m)	[mal]
mountain range	**vargmal** (m)	[vargmál]
mountain ridge	**kresht malor** (m)	[kréʃt malóɾ]

summit, top	**majë** (f)	[májə]
peak	**maja më e lartë** (f)	[mája mə ɛ lártə]
foot (~ of the mountain)	**rrëza e malit** (f)	[rəza ɛ málit]
slope (mountainside)	**shpat** (m)	[ʃpat]

volcano	**vullkan** (m)	[vuɫkán]
active volcano	**vullkan aktiv** (m)	[vuɫkán aktív]
dormant volcano	**vullkan i fjetur** (m)	[vuɫkán i fjétuɾ]

eruption	**shpërthim** (m)	[ʃpəɾθím]
crater	**krater** (m)	[kratér]
magma	**magmë** (f)	[mágmə]
lava	**llavë** (f)	[ɫávə]
molten (~ lava)	**i shkrirë**	[i ʃkríɾə]
canyon	**kanion** (m)	[kanión]
gorge	**grykë** (f)	[grýkə]

| crevice | **çarje** (f) | [tʃárjɛ] |
| abyss (chasm) | **humnerë** (f) | [humnérə] |

pass, col	**kalim** (m)	[kalím]
plateau	**pllajë** (f)	[pɫájə]
cliff	**shkëmb** (m)	[ʃkəmb]
hill	**kodër** (f)	[kódər]

glacier	**akullnajë** (f)	[akuɫnájə]
waterfall	**ujëvarë** (f)	[ujəvárə]
geyser	**gejzer** (m)	[gɛjzér]
lake	**liqen** (m)	[licén]

plain	**fushë** (f)	[fúʃə]
landscape	**peizazh** (m)	[pɛizáʒ]
echo	**jehonë** (f)	[jɛhónə]

alpinist	**alpinist** (m)	[alpiníst]
rock climber	**alpinist shkëmbßinjsh** (m)	[alpiníst ʃkəmbiɲʃ]
to conquer (in climbing)	**pushtoj majën**	[puʃtój májən]
climb (an easy ~)	**ngjitje** (f)	[ɲítjɛ]

80. Mountains names

The Alps	**Alpet** (pl)	[alpét]
Mont Blanc	**Montblanc** (m)	[montblánk]
The Pyrenees	**Pirenejet** (pl)	[pirɛnéjɛt]

The Carpathians	**Karpatet** (m)	[karpátɛt]
The Ural Mountains	**Malet Urale** (pl)	[málɛt urálɛ]
The Caucasus Mountains	**Malet Kaukaze** (pl)	[málɛt kaukázɛ]
Mount Elbrus	**Mali Elbrus** (m)	[máli ɛlbrús]

The Altai Mountains	**Malet Altai** (pl)	[málɛt altái]
The Tian Shan	**Tian Shani** (m)	[tían ʃáni]
The Pamir Mountains	**Malet e Pamirit** (m)	[málɛt ɛ pamírit]
The Himalayas	**Himalajet** (pl)	[himalájɛt]
Mount Everest	**Mali Everest** (m)	[máli ɛvɛrést]

| The Andes | **andet** (pl) | [ándɛt] |
| Mount Kilimanjaro | **Mali Kilimanxharo** (m) | [máli kilimandʒáro] |

81. Rivers

river	**lum** (m)	[lum]
spring (natural source)	**burim** (m)	[burím]
riverbed (river channel)	**shtrat lumi** (m)	[ʃtrat lúmi]
basin (river valley)	**basen** (m)	[basén]

to flow into ...	rrjedh ...	[rjéð ...]
tributary	derdhje (f)	[dérðjɛ]
bank (of river)	breg (m)	[brɛg]

current (stream)	rrymë (f)	[rýmə]
downstream (adv)	rrjedhje e poshtme	[rjéðjɛ ɛ póʃtmɛ]
upstream (adv)	rrjedhje e sipërme	[rjéðjɛ ɛ sípərmɛ]

inundation	vërshim (m)	[vərʃím]
flooding	përmbytje (f)	[pərmbýtjɛ]
to overflow (vi)	vërshon	[vərʃón]
to flood (vt)	përmbytet	[pərmbýtɛt]

| shallow (shoal) | cekëtinë (f) | [tsɛkətínə] |
| rapids | rrjedhë (f) | [rjéðə] |

dam	digë (f)	[dígə]
canal	kanal (m)	[kanál]
reservoir (artificial lake)	rezervuar (m)	[rɛzɛrvuár]
sluice, lock	pendë ujore (f)	[péndə ujórɛ]

water body (pond, etc.)	plan hidrik (m)	[plan hidrík]
swamp (marshland)	kënetë (f)	[kənétə]
bog, marsh	moçal (m)	[motʃál]
whirlpool	vorbull (f)	[vórbuɬ]

stream (brook)	përrua (f)	[pərúa]
drinking (ab. water)	i pijshëm	[i píjʃəm]
fresh (~ water)	i freskët	[i fréskət]

ice	akull (m)	[ákuɬ]
to freeze over	ngrihet	[ŋríhɛt]
(ab. river, etc.)		

82. Rivers' names

| Seine | Sena (f) | [séna] |
| Loire | Loire (f) | [luar] |

Thames	Temza (f)	[témza]
Rhine	Rajnë (m)	[rájnə]
Danube	Danubi (m)	[danúbi]

Volga	Volga (f)	[vólga]
Don	Doni (m)	[dóni]
Lena	Lena (f)	[léna]

Yellow River	Lumi i Verdhë (m)	[lúmi i vérðə]
Yangtze	Jangce (f)	[jaŋtsé]
Mekong	Mekong (m)	[mɛkóŋ]

Ganges	**Gang** (m)	[gaŋ]
Nile River	**Lumi Nil** (m)	[lúmi nil]
Congo River	**Lumi Kongo** (m)	[lúmi kóŋo]
Okavango River	**Lumi Okavango** (m)	[lúmi okaváŋo]
Zambezi River	**Lumi Zambezi** (m)	[lúmi zambézi]
Limpopo River	**Lumi Limpopo** (m)	[lúmi limpópo]
Mississippi River	**Lumi Misisipi** (m)	[lúmi misisípi]

83. Forest

| forest, wood | **pyll** (m) | [pyɬ] |
| forest (as adj) | **pyjor** | [pyjór] |

thick forest	**pyll i ngjeshur** (m)	[pyɬ i ɲɟéʃur]
grove	**zabel** (m)	[zabél]
forest clearing	**lëndinë** (f)	[ləndínə]

| thicket | **pyllëz** (m) | [pýɬəz] |
| scrubland | **shkurre** (f) | [ʃkúrɛ] |

| footpath (troddenpath) | **shteg** (m) | [ʃtɛg] |
| gully | **hon** (m) | [hon] |

tree	**pemë** (f)	[pémə]
leaf	**gjeth** (m)	[ɟɛθ]
leaves (foliage)	**gjethe** (pl)	[ɟéθɛ]

fall of leaves	**rënie e gjetheve** (f)	[rəníɛ ɛ ɟéθɛvɛ]
to fall (ab. leaves)	**bien**	[bíɛn]
top (of the tree)	**maje** (f)	[májɛ]

branch	**degë** (f)	[dégə]
bough	**degë** (f)	[dégə]
bud (on shrub, tree)	**syth** (m)	[syθ]
needle (of pine tree)	**shtiza pishe** (f)	[ʃtíza píʃɛ]
pine cone	**lule pishe** (f)	[lúlɛ píʃɛ]

tree hollow	**zgavër** (f)	[zgávər]
nest	**fole** (f)	[folé]
burrow (animal hole)	**strofull** (f)	[strófuɬ]

trunk	**trung** (m)	[truŋ]
root	**rrënjë** (f)	[réɲə]
bark	**lëvore** (f)	[ləvórɛ]
moss	**myshk** (m)	[myʃk]

to uproot (remove trees or tree stumps)	**shkul**	[ʃkul]
to chop down	**pres**	[prɛs]
to deforest (vt)	**shpyllëzoj**	[ʃpyɬəzój]

tree stump	cung (m)	[tsún]
campfire	zjarr kampingu (m)	[zjar kampíŋu]
forest fire	zjarr në pyll (m)	[zjar nə pyɫ]
to extinguish (vt)	shuaj	[ʃúaj]

forest ranger	roje pyjore (f)	[rójɛ pyjórɛ]
protection	mbrojtje (f)	[mbrójtjɛ]
to protect (~ nature)	mbroj	[mbrój]
poacher	gjahtar i jashtëligjshëm (m)	[ɟahtár i jaʃtəlíɟʃəm]
steel trap	grackë (f)	[grátskə]

| to gather, to pick (vt) | mbledh | [mbléð] |
| to lose one's way | humb rrugën | [húmb rúgən] |

84. Natural resources

natural resources	burime natyrore (pl)	[burímɛ natyrórɛ]
minerals	minerale (pl)	[minɛrálɛ]
deposits	depozita (pl)	[dɛpozíta]
field (e.g., oilfield)	fushë (f)	[fúʃə]

to mine (extract)	nxjerr	[ndzjér]
mining (extraction)	nxjerrje mineralesh (f)	[ndzjérjɛ minɛrálɛʃ]
ore	xehe (f)	[dzéhɛ]
mine (e.g., for coal)	minierë (f)	[miniérə]
shaft (mine ~)	nivel (m)	[nivél]
miner	minator (m)	[minatór]

| gas (natural ~) | gaz (m) | [gaz] |
| gas pipeline | gazsjellës (m) | [gazsjéɫəs] |

oil (petroleum)	naftë (f)	[náftə]
oil pipeline	naftësjellës (f)	[naftəsjéɫəs]
oil well	pus nafte (m)	[pus náftɛ]
derrick (tower)	burim nafte (m)	[burím náftɛ]
tanker	anije-cisternë (f)	[aníjɛ-tsistérnə]

sand	rërë (f)	[rérə]
limestone	gur gëlqeror (m)	[gur gəlcɛrór]
gravel	zhavorr (m)	[ʒavór]
peat	torfë (f)	[tórfə]
clay	argjilë (f)	[arɟílə]
coal	qymyr (m)	[cymýr]

iron (ore)	hekur (m)	[hékur]
gold	ar (m)	[ár]
silver	argjend (m)	[arɟénd]
nickel	nikel (m)	[nikél]
copper	bakër (m)	[bákər]

zinc	**zink** (m)	[zink]
manganese	**mangan** (m)	[maŋán]
mercury	**merkur** (m)	[mɛrkúr]
lead	**plumb** (m)	[plúmb]

mineral	**mineral** (m)	[minɛrál]
crystal	**kristal** (m)	[kristál]
marble	**mermer** (m)	[mɛrmér]
uranium	**uranium** (m)	[uraniúm]

85. Weather

weather	**moti** (m)	[móti]
weather forecast	**parashikimi i motit** (m)	[paraʃikími i mótit]
temperature	**temperaturë** (f)	[tɛmpɛratúrə]
thermometer	**termometër** (m)	[tɛrmométər]
barometer	**barometër** (m)	[barométər]

| humid (adj) | **i lagësht** | [i lágəʃt] |
| humidity | **lagështi** (f) | [lagəʃtí] |

heat (extreme ~)	**vapë** (f)	[vápə]
hot (torrid)	**shumë nxehtë**	[ʃúmə ndzéhtə]
it's hot	**është nxehtë**	[éʃtə ndzéhtə]

| it's warm | **është ngrohtë** | [éʃtə ŋróhtə] |
| warm (moderately hot) | **ngrohtë** | [ŋróhtə] |

| it's cold | **bën ftohtë** | [bən ftóhtə] |
| cold (adj) | **i ftohtë** | [i ftóhtə] |

sun	**diell** (m)	[díɛɫ]
to shine (vi)	**ndriçon**	[ndritʃón]
sunny (day)	**me diell**	[mɛ díɛɫ]
to come up (vi)	**agon**	[agón]
to set (vi)	**perëndon**	[pɛrəndón]

cloud	**re** (f)	[rɛ]
cloudy (adj)	**vranët**	[vránət]
rain cloud	**re shiu** (f)	[rɛ ʃíu]
somber (gloomy)	**vranët**	[vránət]

rain	**shi** (m)	[ʃi]
it's raining	**bie shi**	[bíɛ ʃi]
rainy (~ day, weather)	**me shi**	[mɛ ʃi]
to drizzle (vi)	**shi i imët**	[ʃi i ímət]

pouring rain	**shi litar** (m)	[ʃi litár]
downpour	**stuhi shiu** (f)	[stuhí ʃíu]
heavy (e.g., ~ rain)	**i fortë**	[i fórtə]

| puddle | brakë (f) | [brákə] |
| to get wet (in rain) | lagem | [lágɛm] |

fog (mist)	mjegull (f)	[mjéguɫ]
foggy	e mjegullt	[ɛ mjéguɫt]
snow	borë (f)	[bórə]
it's snowing	bie borë	[bíɛ bórə]

86. Severe weather. Natural disasters

thunderstorm	stuhi (f)	[stuhí]
lightning (~ strike)	vetëtimë (f)	[vɛtətímə]
to flash (vi)	vetëton	[vɛtətón]

thunder	bubullimë (f)	[bubuɫímə]
to thunder (vi)	bubullon	[bubuɫón]
it's thundering	bubullon	[bubuɫón]

| hail | breshër (m) | [bréʃər] |
| it's hailing | po bie breshër | [po bіɛ bréʃər] |

| to flood (vt) | përmbytet | [pərmbýtɛt] |
| flood, inundation | përmbytje (f) | [pərmbýtjɛ] |

earthquake	tërmet (m)	[tərmét]
tremor, shoke	lëkundje (f)	[ləkúndjɛ]
epicenter	epiqendër (f)	[ɛpicéndər]

| eruption | shpërthim (m) | [ʃpərθím] |
| lava | llavë (f) | [ɫávə] |

twister	vorbull (f)	[vórbuɫ]
tornado	tornado (f)	[tornádo]
typhoon	tajfun (m)	[tajfún]

hurricane	uragan (m)	[uragán]
storm	stuhi (f)	[stuhí]
tsunami	cunam (m)	[tsunám]

cyclone	ciklon (m)	[tsiklón]
bad weather	mot i keq (m)	[mot i kɛc]
fire (accident)	zjarr (m)	[zjar]

| disaster | fatkeqësi (f) | [fatkɛcəsí] |
| meteorite | meteor (m) | [mɛtɛór] |

avalanche	ortek (m)	[orték]
snowslide	rrëshqitje bore (f)	[rəʃcítjɛ bórɛ]
blizzard	stuhi bore (f)	[stuhí bórɛ]
snowstorm	stuhi bore (f)	[stuhí bórɛ]

FAUNA

87. Mammals. Predators

predator	grabitqar (m)	[grabitcár]
tiger	tigër (m)	[tígər]
lion	luan (m)	[luán]
wolf	ujk (m)	[ujk]
fox	dhelpër (f)	[ðélpər]
jaguar	jaguar (m)	[jaguár]
leopard	leopard (m)	[lɛopárd]
cheetah	gepard (m)	[gɛpárd]
black panther	panterë e zezë (f)	[pantérə ɛ zézə]
puma	puma (f)	[púma]
snow leopard	leopard i borës (m)	[lɛopárd i bórəs]
lynx	rrëqebull (m)	[rəcébuɫ]
coyote	kojotë (f)	[kojótə]
jackal	çakall (m)	[tʃakáɫ]
hyena	hienë (f)	[hiénə]

88. Wild animals

animal	kafshë (f)	[káfʃə]
beast (animal)	bishë (f)	[bíʃə]
squirrel	ketër (m)	[kétər]
hedgehog	iriq (m)	[iríc]
hare	lepur i egër (m)	[lépur i égər]
rabbit	lepur (m)	[lépur]
badger	vjedull (f)	[vjéduɫ]
raccoon	rakun (m)	[rakún]
hamster	hamster (m)	[hamstér]
marmot	marmot (m)	[marmót]
mole	urith (m)	[uríθ]
mouse	mi (m)	[mi]
rat	mi (m)	[mi]
bat	lakuriq (m)	[lakuríc]
ermine	herminë (f)	[hɛrmínə]
sable	kunadhe (f)	[kunáðɛ]

marten	shqarth (m)	[ʃcarθ]
weasel	nuselalë (f)	[nusɛlálə]
mink	vizon (m)	[vizón]

| beaver | kastor (m) | [kastór] |
| otter | vidër (f) | [vídər] |

horse	kali (m)	[káli]
moose	dre brilopatë (m)	[drɛ brilopátə]
deer	dre (f)	[drɛ]
camel	deve (f)	[dévɛ]

bison	bizon (m)	[bizón]
wisent	bizon evropian (m)	[bizón ɛvropián]
buffalo	buall (m)	[búaɫ]

zebra	zebër (f)	[zébər]
antelope	antilopë (f)	[antilópə]
roe deer	dre (f)	[drɛ]
fallow deer	dre ugar (m)	[drɛ ugár]
chamois	kamosh (m)	[kamóʃ]
wild boar	derr i egër (m)	[dér i égər]

whale	balenë (f)	[balénə]
seal	fokë (f)	[fókə]
walrus	lopë deti (f)	[lópə déti]
fur seal	fokë (f)	[fókə]
dolphin	delfin (m)	[dɛlfín]

bear	ari (m)	[arí]
polar bear	ari polar (m)	[arí polár]
panda	panda (f)	[pánda]

monkey	majmun (m)	[majmún]
chimpanzee	shimpanze (f)	[ʃimpánzɛ]
orangutan	orangutan (m)	[oraŋután]
gorilla	gorillë (f)	[goríɫə]
macaque	majmun makao (m)	[majmún makáo]
gibbon	gibon (m)	[gibón]

elephant	elefant (m)	[ɛlɛfánt]
rhinoceros	rinoqeront (m)	[rinocɛrónt]
giraffe	gjirafë (f)	[ɟiráfə]
hippopotamus	hipopotam (m)	[hipopotám]

| kangaroo | kangur (m) | [kaŋúr] |
| koala (bear) | koala (f) | [koála] |

mongoose	mangustë (f)	[maŋústə]
chinchilla	çinçila (f)	[tʃintʃíla]
skunk	qelbës (m)	[célbəs]
porcupine	ferrëgjatë (m)	[fɛrəɟátə]

89. Domestic animals

cat	mace (f)	[mátsɛ]
tomcat	maçok (m)	[matʃók]
dog	qen (m)	[cɛn]
horse	kali (m)	[káli]
stallion (male horse)	hamshor (m)	[hamʃór]
mare	pelë (f)	[pélə]
cow	lopë (f)	[lópə]
bull	dem (m)	[dém]
ox	ka (m)	[ka]
sheep (ewe)	dele (f)	[délɛ]
ram	dash (m)	[daʃ]
goat	dhi (f)	[ði]
billy goat, he-goat	cjap (m)	[tsjáp]
donkey	gomar (m)	[gomár]
mule	mushkë (f)	[múʃkə]
pig, hog	derr (m)	[dɛr]
piglet	derrkuc (m)	[dɛrkúts]
rabbit	lepur (m)	[lépur]
hen (chicken)	pulë (f)	[púlə]
rooster	gjel (m)	[ɟél]
duck	rosë (f)	[rósə]
drake	rosak (m)	[rosák]
goose	patë (f)	[pátə]
tom turkey, gobbler	gjel deti i egër (m)	[ɟél déti i égər]
turkey (hen)	gjel deti (m)	[ɟél déti]
domestic animals	kafshë shtëpiake (f)	[káfʃə ʃtəpiákɛ]
tame (e.g., ~ hamster)	i zbutur	[i zbútur]
to tame (vt)	zbus	[zbus]
to breed (vt)	rrit	[rit]
farm	fermë (f)	[férmə]
poultry	pulari (f)	[pularí]
cattle	bagëti (f)	[bagətí]
herd (cattle)	kope (f)	[kopé]
stable	stallë (f)	[stáɫə]
pigpen	stallë e derrave (f)	[stáɫə ɛ déravɛ]
cowshed	stallë e lopëve (f)	[stáɫə ɛ lópəvɛ]
rabbit hutch	kolibe lepujsh (f)	[kolíbɛ lépujʃ]
hen house	kotec (m)	[kotéts]

90. Birds

bird	zog (m)	[zog]
pigeon	pëllumb (m)	[pətúmb]
sparrow	harabel (m)	[harabél]
tit (great tit)	xhixhimës (m)	[dʒidʒimés]
magpie	laraskë (f)	[laráskə]

raven	korb (m)	[korb]
crow	sorrë (f)	[sórə]
jackdaw	galë (f)	[gálə]
rook	sorrë (f)	[sórə]

duck	rosë (f)	[rósə]
goose	patë (f)	[pátə]
pheasant	fazan (m)	[fazán]

eagle	shqiponjë (f)	[ʃcipóɲə]
hawk	gjeraqinë (f)	[ɟɛracínə]
falcon	fajkua (f)	[fajkúa]
vulture	hutë (f)	[hútə]
condor (Andean ~)	kondor (m)	[kondór]

swan	mjellmë (f)	[mjétmə]
crane	lejlek (m)	[lɛjlék]
stork	lejlek (m)	[lɛjlék]

parrot	papagall (m)	[papagáɫ]
hummingbird	kolibri (m)	[kolíbri]
peacock	pallua (m)	[paɫúa]

ostrich	struc (m)	[struts]
heron	çafkë (f)	[tʃáfkə]
flamingo	flamingo (m)	[flamíŋo]
pelican	pelikan (m)	[pɛlikán]

| nightingale | bilbil (m) | [bilbíl] |
| swallow | dallëndyshe (f) | [daɫəndýʃɛ] |

thrush	mëllenjë (f)	[mətéɲə]
song thrush	grifsha (f)	[grífʃa]
blackbird	mëllenjë (f)	[mətéɲə]

swift	dallëndyshe (f)	[daɫəndýʃɛ]
lark	thëllëzë (f)	[θətə́zə]
quail	trumcak (m)	[trumtsák]

woodpecker	qukapik (m)	[cukapík]
cuckoo	kukuvajkë (f)	[kukuvájkə]
owl	buf (m)	[buf]
eagle owl	buf mbretëror (m)	[buf mbrɛtərór]

wood grouse	**fazan i pyllit** (m)	[fazán i pýłit]
black grouse	**fazan i zi** (m)	[fazán i zí]
partridge	**thëllëzë** (f)	[θǝłǝ́zǝ]
starling	**gargull** (m)	[gárguł]
canary	**kanarinë** (f)	[kanarínǝ]
hazel grouse	**fazan mali** (m)	[fazán máli]
chaffinch	**trishtil** (m)	[triʃtíl]
bullfinch	**trishtil dimri** (m)	[triʃtíl dímri]
seagull	**pulëbardhë** (f)	[pulǝbárðǝ]
albatross	**albatros** (m)	[albatrós]
penguin	**penguin** (m)	[pɛŋuín]

91. Fish. Marine animals

bream	**krapuliq** (m)	[krapulíc]
carp	**krap** (m)	[krap]
perch	**perç** (m)	[pɛrtʃ]
catfish	**mustak** (m)	[musták]
pike	**mlysh** (m)	[mlýʃ]
salmon	**salmon** (m)	[salmón]
sturgeon	**bli** (m)	[blí]
herring	**harengë** (f)	[harénǝ]
Atlantic salmon	**salmon Atlantiku** (m)	[salmón atlantíku]
mackerel	**skumbri** (m)	[skúmbri]
flatfish	**shojzë** (f)	[ʃójzǝ]
zander, pike perch	**troftë** (f)	[tróftǝ]
cod	**merluc** (m)	[mɛrlúts]
tuna	**tunë** (f)	[túnǝ]
trout	**troftë** (f)	[tróftǝ]
eel	**ngjalë** (f)	[nɟálǝ]
electric ray	**peshk elektrik** (m)	[pɛʃk ɛlɛktrík]
moray eel	**ngjalë morel** (f)	[nɟálǝ morél]
piranha	**piranja** (f)	[piráɲa]
shark	**peshkaqen** (m)	[pɛʃkacén]
dolphin	**delfin** (m)	[dɛlfín]
whale	**balenë** (f)	[balénǝ]
crab	**gaforre** (f)	[gafórɛ]
jellyfish	**kandil deti** (m)	[kandíl déti]
octopus	**oktapod** (m)	[oktapód]
starfish	**yll deti** (m)	[yɫ déti]
sea urchin	**iriq deti** (m)	[iríc déti]

seahorse	kalë deti (m)	[kálə déti]
oyster	midhje (f)	[míðjɛ]
shrimp	karkalec (m)	[karkaléts]
lobster	karavidhe (f)	[karavíðɛ]
spiny lobster	karavidhe (f)	[karavíðɛ]

92. Amphibians. Reptiles

snake	gjarpër (m)	[ɟárpər]
venomous (snake)	helmues	[hɛlmúɛs]

viper	nepërka (f)	[nɛpérka]
cobra	kobra (f)	[kóbra]
python	piton (m)	[pitón]
boa	boa (f)	[bóa]

grass snake	kular (m)	[kulár]
rattle snake	gjarpër me zile (m)	[ɟárpər mɛ zílɛ]
anaconda	anakonda (f)	[anakónda]

lizard	hardhucë (f)	[harðútsə]
iguana	iguana (f)	[iguána]
monitor lizard	varan (m)	[varán]
salamander	salamandër (f)	[salamándər]
chameleon	kameleon (m)	[kamɛlɛón]
scorpion	akrep (m)	[akrép]

turtle	breshkë (f)	[bréʃkə]
frog	bretkosë (f)	[brɛtkósə]
toad	zhabë (f)	[ʒábə]
crocodile	krokodil (m)	[krokodíl]

93. Insects

insect, bug	insekt (m)	[insékt]
butterfly	flutur (f)	[flútur]
ant	milingonë (f)	[miliŋónə]
fly	mizë (f)	[mízə]
mosquito	mushkonjë (f)	[muʃkóɲə]
beetle	brumbull (m)	[brúmbuɫ]

wasp	grerëz (f)	[grérəz]
bee	bletë (f)	[blétə]
bumblebee	greth (m)	[grɛθ]
gadfly (botfly)	zekth (m)	[zɛkθ]

spider	merimangë (f)	[mɛrimáŋə]
spiderweb	rrjetë merimange (f)	[rjétə mɛrimáŋɛ]

dragonfly	**pilivesë** (f)	[pilivésə]
grasshopper	**karkalec** (m)	[karkaléts]
moth (night butterfly)	**molë** (f)	[mólə]
cockroach	**kacabu** (f)	[katsabú]
tick	**rriqër** (m)	[rícər]
flea	**plesht** (m)	[plɛʃt]
midge	**mushicë** (f)	[muʃítsə]
locust	**gjinkallë** (f)	[ɟinkáɬə]
snail	**kërmill** (m)	[kərmíɬ]
cricket	**bulkth** (m)	[búlkθ]
lightning bug	**xixëllonjë** (f)	[dzidzəɫóɲə]
ladybug	**mollëkuqe** (f)	[moɫəkúcɛ]
cockchafer	**vizhë** (f)	[víʒə]
leech	**shushunjë** (f)	[ʃuʃúɲə]
caterpillar	**vemje** (f)	[vémjɛ]
earthworm	**krimb toke** (m)	[krímb tókɛ]
larva	**larvë** (f)	[lárvə]

FLORA

94. Trees

tree	**pemë** (f)	[pémə]
deciduous (adj)	**gjethor**	[ɟɛθór]
coniferous (adj)	**halor**	[halór]
evergreen (adj)	**përherë të gjelbra**	[pərhérə tə ɟélbra]
apple tree	**pemë molle** (f)	[pémə mótɛ]
pear tree	**pemë dardhe** (f)	[pémə dárðɛ]
sweet cherry tree	**pemë qershie** (f)	[pémə cɛrʃíɛ]
sour cherry tree	**pemë qershi vishnje** (f)	[pémə cɛrʃí víʃɲɛ]
plum tree	**pemë kumbulle** (f)	[pémə kúmbutɛ]
birch	**mështekna** (f)	[məʃtékna]
oak	**lis** (m)	[lis]
linden tree	**bli** (m)	[blí]
aspen	**plep i egër** (m)	[plɛp i égər]
maple	**panjë** (f)	[páɲə]
spruce	**bredh** (m)	[brɛð]
pine	**pishë** (f)	[píʃə]
larch	**larsh** (m)	[lárʃ]
fir tree	**bredh i bardhë** (m)	[brɛð i bárðə]
cedar	**kedër** (m)	[kédər]
poplar	**plep** (m)	[plɛp]
rowan	**vadhë** (f)	[váðə]
willow	**shelg** (m)	[ʃɛlg]
alder	**verr** (m)	[vɛr]
beech	**ah** (m)	[ah]
elm	**elm** (m)	[élm]
ash (tree)	**shelg** (m)	[ʃɛlg]
chestnut	**gështenjë** (f)	[gəʃtéɲə]
magnolia	**manjolia** (f)	[maɲólia]
palm tree	**palma** (f)	[pálma]
cypress	**qiparis** (m)	[ciparís]
mangrove	**rizoforë** (f)	[rizofórə]
baobab	**baobab** (m)	[baobáb]
eucalyptus	**eukalipt** (m)	[ɛukalípt]
sequoia	**sekuojë** (f)	[sɛkuójə]

95. Shrubs

bush	**shkurre** (f)	[ʃkúrɛ]
shrub	**kaçube** (f)	[katʃúbɛ]
grapevine	**hardhi** (f)	[harðí]
vineyard	**vreshtë** (f)	[vréʃtə]
raspberry bush	**mjedër** (f)	[mjédər]
blackcurrant bush	**kaliboba e zezë** (f)	[kalibóba ɛ zézə]
redcurrant bush	**kaliboba e kuqe** (f)	[kalibóba ɛ kúcɛ]
gooseberry bush	**shkurre kulumbrie** (f)	[ʃkúrɛ kulumbríɛ]
acacia	**akacie** (f)	[akátsiɛ]
barberry	**krespinë** (f)	[krɛspínə]
jasmine	**jasemin** (m)	[jasɛmín]
juniper	**dëllinjë** (f)	[dəɫíɲə]
rosebush	**trëndafil** (m)	[trəndafíl]
dog rose	**trëndafil i egër** (m)	[trəndafíl i égər]

96. Fruits. Berries

fruit	**frut** (m)	[frut]
fruits	**fruta** (pl)	[frúta]
apple	**mollë** (f)	[móɫə]
pear	**dardhë** (f)	[dárðə]
plum	**kumbull** (f)	[kúmbuɫ]
strawberry (garden ~)	**luleshtrydhe** (f)	[lulɛʃtrýðɛ]
sour cherry	**qershi vishnje** (f)	[cɛrʃí víʃɲɛ]
sweet cherry	**qershi** (f)	[cɛrʃí]
grape	**rrush** (m)	[ruʃ]
raspberry	**mjedër** (f)	[mjédər]
blackcurrant	**kaliboba e zezë** (f)	[kalibóba ɛ zézə]
redcurrant	**kaliboba e kuqe** (f)	[kalibóba ɛ kúcɛ]
gooseberry	**kulumbri** (f)	[kulumbrí]
cranberry	**boronica** (f)	[boronítsa]
orange	**portokall** (m)	[portokáɫ]
mandarin	**mandarinë** (f)	[mandarínə]
pineapple	**ananas** (m)	[ananás]
banana	**banane** (f)	[banánɛ]
date	**hurmë** (f)	[húrmə]
lemon	**limon** (m)	[limón]
apricot	**kajsi** (f)	[kajsí]

peach	pjeshkë (f)	[pjéʃkə]
kiwi	kivi (m)	[kívi]
grapefruit	grejpfrut (m)	[grɛjpfrút]

berry	manë (f)	[mánə]
berries	mana (f)	[mána]
cowberry	boronicë mirtile (f)	[boronítsə mirtílɛ]
wild strawberry	luleshtrydhe e egër (f)	[lulɛʃtrýðɛ ɛ égər]
bilberry	boronicë (f)	[boronítsə]

97. Flowers. Plants

| flower | lule (f) | [lúlɛ] |
| bouquet (of flowers) | buqetë (f) | [bucétə] |

rose (flower)	trëndafil (m)	[trəndafíl]
tulip	tulipan (m)	[tulipán]
carnation	karafil (m)	[karafíl]
gladiolus	gladiolë (f)	[gladiólə]

cornflower	lule misri (f)	[lúlɛ mísri]
harebell	lule këmborë (f)	[lúlɛ kəmbórə]
dandelion	luleradhiqe (f)	[lulɛraðícɛ]
camomile	kamomil (m)	[kamomíl]

aloe	aloe (f)	[alóɛ]
cactus	kaktus (m)	[kaktús]
rubber plant, ficus	fikus (m)	[fíkus]

lily	zambak (m)	[zambák]
geranium	barbarozë (f)	[barbarózə]
hyacinth	zymbyl (m)	[zymbýl]

mimosa	mimoza (f)	[mimóza]
narcissus	narcis (m)	[nartsís]
nasturtium	lule këmbore (f)	[lúlɛ kəmbórɛ]

orchid	orkide (f)	[orkidé]
peony	bozhure (f)	[boʒúrɛ]
violet	vjollcë (f)	[vjóɫtsə]

pansy	lule vjollca (f)	[lúlɛ vjóɫtsa]
forget-me-not	mosmëharro (f)	[mosməharó]
daisy	margaritë (f)	[margarítə]

poppy	lulëkuqe (f)	[luləkúcɛ]
hemp	kërp (m)	[kərp]
mint	mendër (f)	[méndər]
lily of the valley	zambak i fushës (m)	[zambák i fúʃəs]
snowdrop	luleborë (f)	[lulɛbórə]

nettle	**hithra** (f)	[híθra]
sorrel	**lëpjeta** (f)	[ləpjéta]
water lily	**zambak uji** (m)	[zambák új¡]
fern	**fier** (m)	[fíɛr]
lichen	**likene** (f)	[likénɛ]

conservatory (greenhouse)	**serrë** (f)	[sérə]
lawn	**lëndinë** (f)	[ləndínə]
flowerbed	**kënd lulishteje** (m)	[kənd lulíʃtɛjɛ]

plant	**bimë** (f)	[bímə]
grass	**bar** (m)	[bar]
blade of grass	**fije bari** (f)	[fíjɛ bári]

leaf	**gjeth** (m)	[ɟɛθ]
petal	**petale** (f)	[pɛtálɛ]
stem	**bisht** (m)	[biʃt]
tuber	**zhardhok** (m)	[ʒarðók]

young plant (shoot)	**filiz** (m)	[filíz]
thorn	**gjemb** (m)	[ɟémb]

to blossom (vi)	**lulëzoj**	[luləzój]
to fade, to wither	**vyshket**	[výʃkɛt]
smell (odor)	**aromë** (f)	[arómə]
to cut (flowers)	**pres lulet**	[prɛs lúlɛt]
to pick (a flower)	**mbledh lule**	[mbléð lúlɛ]

98. Cereals, grains

grain	**drithë** (m)	[dríθə]
cereal crops	**drithëra** (pl)	[dríθəra]
ear (of barley, etc.)	**kaush** (m)	[kaúʃ]

wheat	**grurë** (f)	[grúrə]
rye	**thekër** (f)	[θékər]
oats	**tërshërë** (f)	[tərʃérə]

millet	**mel** (m)	[mɛl]
barley	**elb** (m)	[ɛlb]

corn	**misër** (m)	[mísər]
rice	**oriz** (m)	[oríz]
buckwheat	**hikërr** (m)	[híkər]

pea plant	**bizele** (f)	[bizélɛ]
kidney bean	**groshë** (f)	[gróʃə]
soy	**sojë** (f)	[sójə]
lentil	**thjerrëz** (f)	[θjérəz]
beans (pulse crops)	**fasule** (f)	[fasúlɛ]

COUNTRIES OF THE WORLD

99. Countries. Part 1

Afghanistan	**Afganistan** (m)	[afganistán]
Albania	**Shqipëri** (f)	[ʃcipərí]
Argentina	**Argjentinë** (f)	[arɟɛntínə]
Armenia	**Armeni** (f)	[armɛní]
Australia	**Australia** (f)	[australía]
Austria	**Austri** (f)	[austrí]
Azerbaijan	**Azerbajxhan** (m)	[azɛrbajdʒán]
The Bahamas	**Bahamas** (m)	[bahámas]
Bangladesh	**Bangladesh** (m)	[baŋladéʃ]
Belarus	**Bjellorusi** (f)	[bjɛłorusí]
Belgium	**Belgjikë** (f)	[bɛlɟíkə]
Bolivia	**Bolivi** (f)	[boliví]
Bosnia and Herzegovina	**Bosnje Herzegovina** (f)	[bósɲɛ hɛrzɛgovína]
Brazil	**Brazil** (m)	[brazíl]
Bulgaria	**Bullgari** (f)	[buɫgarí]
Cambodia	**Kamboxhia** (f)	[kambódʒia]
Canada	**Kanada** (f)	[kanadá]
Chile	**Kili** (m)	[kíli]
China	**Kinë** (f)	[kínə]
Colombia	**Kolumbi** (f)	[kolumbí]
Croatia	**Kroaci** (f)	[kroatsí]
Cuba	**Kuba** (f)	[kúba]
Cyprus	**Qipro** (f)	[cípro]
Czech Republic	**Republika Çeke** (f)	[rɛpublíka tʃékɛ]
Denmark	**Danimarkë** (f)	[danimárkə]
Dominican Republic	**Republika Dominikane** (f)	[rɛpublíka dominikánɛ]
Ecuador	**Ekuador** (m)	[ɛkuadór]
Egypt	**Egjipt** (m)	[ɛɟípt]
England	**Angli** (f)	[aŋlí]
Estonia	**Estoni** (f)	[ɛstoní]
Finland	**Finlandë** (f)	[finlándə]
France	**Francë** (f)	[frántsə]
French Polynesia	**Polinezia Franceze** (f)	[polinɛzía frantsézɛ]
Georgia	**Gjeorgji** (f)	[ɟɛorɟí]
Germany	**Gjermani** (f)	[ɟɛrmaní]
Ghana	**Gana** (f)	[gána]
Great Britain	**Britani e Madhe** (f)	[brítani ɛ máðɛ]
Greece	**Greqi** (f)	[grɛcí]

| Haiti | **Haiti** (m) | [haíti] |
| Hungary | **Hungari** (f) | [huŋarí] |

100. Countries. Part 2

Iceland	**Islandë** (f)	[islándə]
India	**Indi** (f)	[indí]
Indonesia	**Indonezi** (f)	[indonɛzí]
Iran	**Iran** (m)	[irán]
Iraq	**Irak** (m)	[irak]
Ireland	**Irlandë** (f)	[irlándə]
Israel	**Izrael** (m)	[izraél]
Italy	**Itali** (f)	[italí]

Jamaica	**Xhamajka** (f)	[dʒamájka]
Japan	**Japoni** (f)	[japoní]
Jordan	**Jordani** (f)	[jordaní]
Kazakhstan	**Kazakistan** (m)	[kazakistán]
Kenya	**Kenia** (f)	[kénia]
Kirghizia	**Kirgistan** (m)	[kirgistán]
Kuwait	**Kuvajt** (m)	[kuvájt]

Laos	**Laos** (m)	[láos]
Latvia	**Letoni** (f)	[lɛtoní]
Lebanon	**Liban** (m)	[libán]
Libya	**Libia** (f)	[libía]
Liechtenstein	**Lichtenstein** (m)	[litshtɛnstéin]
Lithuania	**Lituani** (f)	[lituaní]
Luxembourg	**Luksemburg** (m)	[luksɛmbúrg]

Macedonia (Republic of ~)	**Maqedonia** (f)	[macɛdonía]
Madagascar	**Madagaskar** (m)	[madagaskár]
Malaysia	**Malajzi** (f)	[malajzí]
Malta	**Maltë** (f)	[máltə]
Mexico	**Meksikë** (f)	[mɛksíkə]
Moldova, Moldavia	**Moldavi** (f)	[moldaví]

Monaco	**Monako** (f)	[monáko]
Mongolia	**Mongoli** (f)	[moŋolí]
Montenegro	**Mali i Zi** (m)	[máli i zí]

| Morocco | **Marok** (m) | [marók] |
| Myanmar | **Mianmar** (m) | [mianmár] |

Namibia	**Namibia** (f)	[namíbia]
Nepal	**Nepal** (m)	[nɛpál]
Netherlands	**Holandë** (f)	[holándə]
New Zealand	**Zelandë e Re** (f)	[zɛlándə ɛ ré]
North Korea	**Korea e Veriut** (f)	[koréa ɛ vériut]
Norway	**Norvegji** (f)	[norvɛɟí]

101. Countries. Part 3

Pakistan	**Pakistan** (m)	[pakistán]
Palestine	**Palestinë** (f)	[palɛstínə]
Panama	**Panama** (f)	[panamá]
Paraguay	**Paraguai** (m)	[paraguái]
Peru	**Peru** (f)	[pɛrú]
Poland	**Poloni** (f)	[poloní]
Portugal	**Portugali** (f)	[portugalí]
Romania	**Rumani** (f)	[rumaní]
Russia	**Rusi** (f)	[rusí]
Saudi Arabia	**Arabia Saudite** (f)	[arabía saudítɛ]
Scotland	**Skoci** (f)	[skotsí]
Senegal	**Senegal** (m)	[sɛnɛgál]
Serbia	**Serbi** (f)	[sɛrbí]
Slovakia	**Sllovaki** (f)	[słovakí]
Slovenia	**Sllovenia** (f)	[słovɛnía]
South Africa	**Afrika e Jugut** (f)	[afríka ɛ júgut]
South Korea	**Korea e Jugut** (f)	[koréa ɛ júgut]
Spain	**Spanjë** (f)	[spáɲə]
Suriname	**Surinam** (m)	[surinám]
Sweden	**Suedi** (f)	[suɛdí]
Switzerland	**Zvicër** (f)	[zvítsər]
Syria	**Siri** (f)	[sirí]
Taiwan	**Tajvan** (m)	[tajván]
Tajikistan	**Taxhikistan** (m)	[tadʒikistán]
Tanzania	**Tanzani** (f)	[tanzaní]
Tasmania	**Tasmani** (f)	[tasmaní]
Thailand	**Tajlandë** (f)	[tajlándə]
Tunisia	**Tunizi** (f)	[tunizí]
Turkey	**Turqi** (f)	[turcí]
Turkmenistan	**Turkmenistan** (m)	[turkmɛnistán]
Ukraine	**Ukrainë** (f)	[ukraínə]
United Arab Emirates	**Emiratet e Bashkuara Arabe** (pl)	[ɛmirátɛt ɛ baʃkúara arábɛ]
United States of America	**Shtetet e Bashkuara të Amerikës**	[ʃtétɛt ɛ baʃkúara tə amɛríkəs]
Uruguay	**Uruguai** (m)	[uruguái]
Uzbekistan	**Uzbekistan** (m)	[uzbɛkistán]
Vatican	**Vatikan** (m)	[vatikán]
Venezuela	**Venezuelë** (f)	[vɛnɛzuélə]
Vietnam	**Vietnam** (m)	[viɛtnám]
Zanzibar	**Zanzibar** (m)	[zanzibár]